In Memory *of the*
Grumpy Old Man

In Memory *of the*
Grumpy Old Man

A Political Point of View From a Very Common Person

B. MICHAEL MORO

Order this book online at www.trafford.com
or email orders@trafford.com

Most Trafford titles are also available at major online book retailers.

Printed in the United States of America.

ISBN: 978-1-4669-0616-7 (sc)
ISBN: 978-1-4669-0618-1 (hc)
ISBN: 978-1-4669-0617-4 (e)

Library of Congress Control Number: 2011961566

Trafford rev. 1/13/2012

 www.trafford.com

North America & international
toll-free: 1 888 232 4444 (USA & Canada)
phone: 250 383 6864 ◆ fax: 812 355 4082

Table of Contents

To say goodbye to someone can be a very difficult thing to do, especially when you have known someone for most of your life. I have known the Grumpy Old Man for that long. Though we have shared several points of view, we also didn't with half as many. Even came close to a fist fight or two on a couple of occasions. I guess we were close enough for him to trust me with his anonymity after he took me up on my sarcastic comment that he should open up a website to voice his opinions, and believe me, he was opinionated.

When he passed away it was as though no one had noticed. The winter was ending, spring rains helped to melt away the snow, the world politics went on as usual, and even his own family didn't seem to miss him as much as I perhaps did. It wasn't that he was such a miserable person and nobody liked him, he did have a tendency to rub people the wrong way by pointing out their faults, but it was as though he had just faded away.

I had told him that he should spread his opinions over the internet, perhaps with a website, and he conned me into helping him. I even paid for it to get him out of my hair and into something that would preoccupy him enough to keep him there, but he still kept conning me into helping him upload his messages to his website. In the end, he never got to say all that he had to say, and it's a shame. He had a lot to say and a lot of it was good things too.

When I promised him that I would keep his real name a secret I didn't expect him to go so soon, but out of respect I still am willing to keep my promise. As a friend, we shared some thoughts and concerns, some ideas and some comments about others, and I suppose that a little part of him is still left in me.

In retrospect, there is a little of the Grumpy Old Man in all of us. As you consider this and as you read further on, I know you will think about your own life and points of view on the subject material ahead. Any statements can be found in most Encyclopedias. I'm sure there have been many of times where you have thought about something that deeply caught your interests and you formed an opinion on. I will even bet you as an individual that you even considered what the perfect world would be like, even going as far as taking what you have to work with and changing it for the better.

So, to give him the tribute that I owe him and some of what he so deserves, it is my honor to give you his thoughts, his opinions, and his comments. I give you The Grumpy Old Man.

I am The Grumpy Old Man

I HAVE BEEN around for awhile. I am old enough to have fought in the Viet Nam war. I was around when a Good President was assassinated and a world mourned and conspiracies abounded, and I have seen Presidents that were not as good. I remember watching on television, the Beatles performing on "The Ed Sullivan Show" for the first time, even though I complained to my sister that I would rather watch "The Wonderful World of Disney". Our only television was used, black and white, and we could only get channels' Three and Six, and that was with an antennae mounted to the roof with a rotor to turn the antennae into the right direction. I use to listen to the Yankees and the Red Sox playing their games on the radio with my Dad and my Grandfather. I spent a good part of my life trying to save the world, traveling half way around the world and back a few times, and finding out later that you can't save something that doesn't want to be saved.

In retrospect, I have seen a lot of life, in every shape and form, some good and some not so good. I've seen babies' born, and young and old die. I've shed tears for the loss of a good person, and I usually root for the underdog. I'm constantly trying to find the middle ground and understanding all sides to the problem. Though to my peers I may seem a bit of a complainer, but I am only trying to find the best solution for all that are involved. I strongly feel that to understand completely the problem, a common ground can finally be achieved. I have witnessed far too often, the many times people carrying on and on, "half cocked" as it seems, about an issue without knowing any of the dynamics that made the situation or problem exist in the first place. Opinions are respected, but to what point do we keep going in the wrong direction with them?

Some of my issues are centered in and around the area where I live and grew up, as well as places I have visited and places I had worked in various parts of the world. Unlike most people, I take the time to listen. What people say is very important. The average person does care about the world that they live in and should have a say in how it is run. If my comments offend you, then I apologize. If my attitude and outspoken words seem offensive, again, I apologize. I was raised to not pull my punches and shoot straight from the hip. If you agree with me, then stick to your guns and pass the message on.

In the following thoughts, my comments are always geared around being fair and just, to all concerned. I look at a situation and try to find the history that led up to the situation, seeing what all side's concerns are based upon. Then, a solution can be formed that is fair to all who are directly involved. I believe in being upfront and honest and I'm not one to pull too many punches.

Supposedly, this country was based upon equality (though it actually wasn't), and though I seem to be condemning the wealthy, but actually I am only condemning the very wealthy. Ever since man stepped into the first steps towards being civilized, power has been the driving force that made individuals step up and take charge, so to say. Power is wealth, and the more wealth one has the more power comes with it. It is as simple as that. The most wealthy have the most power, and as the story goes, to keep and increase one's power, one will go to extremes, even decide on who lives and who dies to gain that extra wealth, and even more power. That is power, hence that is wealth. Every war was fought for the keeping of power and usually to acquire more wealth with the final outcome. "To the victor go the spoils." It is a plain and simple fact about human history. Wealth runs the world.

Keep in mind that the world may seem to revolve around the whims of wealth, but if it weren't for the strong backs of the not so wealthy, the common person whom are the overwhelming majority, this big world would not revolve, and that is whom I seek a level playing field for, the majority. There lies the problems of the world and in there are the solutions. So, for the wealthy, be grateful that there are those of us who do the work that you, the wealthy minority, feel it is beneath you. Think of all the things that make your life continue on and all of those little things that someone else does for you that you would not be caught dead doing.

When I was a young man I remember hearing people talking about having to hide some of their earnings. They would state that if they earned up to a certain amount then they would be in a higher tax bracket. This, to me would mean that the more you earn the higher percentage of taxes you would be paying into the Government. Basically, you would be paying a higher price to become wealthier than you are. Somewhere along the way this paying a higher percentage of taxes for the more you earned, has disappeared somewhere. When and where did it go? Was it ever really there?

Everyone should pay their fair share of taxes and everyone should hold themselves accountable, no exceptions and no more loopholes! Big businesses like the oil companies, companies like General Electric, Halliburton, should be paying their fair share and not getting huge tax breaks. Most of these companies were built from the pockets of the average American, the biggest consumers. When a company threatens to move their operations elsewhere if they don't get a huge tax break, it sounds a little like "stronghold tactics" to me. Something that organized crime syndicates would do, which I believe is against the laws of our Great Nation.

For those that are wealthy and are at least earning $250,000 and up, should accept their responsibility and start giving back their fair share. The money you earned did come at a price, and it was on the backs of those who do not earn as much. Wealth is a privilege, not a right, so pay a higher percentage than the lesser privileged. Keep in mind that if the majority of the working class decides they have had enough and refuse to work anymore, then the wealthy minority will suffer worse. Think about it. Who will do all of the jobs you don't have to do and don't want to do? You owe it to pay a higher percentage of taxes, and cut out all of those deductions that your wealth makes it easier for you to do.

I'm tired of hearing the crap that the wealthy are the only ones that can bump start the economy with their tax credits. The majority of the money spent in this country is spent by the common person. When that person has no money to spend, that is when we have a recession.

The economy is based around the home, whether owning or renting. When money is tight, a person's basic needs become that much more important, food, shelter, and comfort from the weather. Even the homeless consider their little shelter from the elements their home. A person's lifestyle, how they live their life from day to day, is their comfort zone. Disrupt their lifestyle, and they fall out of their comfort zone, and people will do almost anything to get back to their comfort zone.

Though the Human Specie has evolved to be the most civilized in our Earth's history, we are still animals by continuing the survival practices of the strong survive and the weak perish. The strong usually picks on the weak. Strong doesn't necessarily mean muscle strength. Intelligence can be the strong factor to survival, adapting to situations by intelligent thought. All in all, it has been the quest of greed that has separated the Human Specie from the animal world, and this practice is what causes the social problems we have faced throughout our time. If you look throughout our history you can see the root cause of all of our problems is based on greed. Some wars may be for the survival of a culture, but its root cause is that of greed, it may be for wealth, for power and control, but it still is greed.

Are We Free?

THIS IS AN argument that my friend the plumber loves to argue about. No, he's not "Joe the Plumber". He is a licensed plumber and a hard working, fare, and honest individual that has a "common sense" way of looking at most things. This is how he says he approaches trouble shooting a problem, by breaking it down into its simplest form and taking it one step at a time. I've heard others comment that he is very meticulous.

I have heard him "trouble shoot" the Revolutionary War in this manner. In his basic words he asks, "Who had the most to lose by the heavy taxation of the American Colonies? Who had the most to gain by eliminating the heavy control of Britain over the American Colonies?"

If you looked at the perspective of the poor dirt farmer, the logger working for the timber company, the trapper, the average common worker, and it also applies to today's similarities, these people made up the workforce and are the majority of the people. Keep in mind that when the colonists first started settling here in the New World they saw a vast virgin forest. Logging became the first and largest industry in the New World because it was a very large natural resource that was exported back to Europe by thousands of boatloads. Europe had almost clear cut their forests and here in the New World were very large, straight trees perfect for ship masts and for building ships and homes. You might say that our trees were the first natural resource to be pilfered by the Europeans.

The large land owners, the timber company owners, the larger shop owners, those that had the investments in businesses that gave them good profits, these people were the minority and had the most to lose. They were the ones that paid the highest percentages of taxes to England. These were the ones that did the most complaining.

The majority didn't have that much to lose. They were glad to be out of poverty struck Europe. At least here in America they could venture out into the wilderness and have a chance to strike it rich or simply disappear out of British sight. There was plenty of wild game to hunt, plenty of land that had been cleared already and could be homesteaded and farmed. All they had to do was not piss off the natives.

Now if you were one of those that were of the minority, one of those that had a lot to lose, and you had opened up your mouth as a group and were getting into trouble with Britain for it, how would you get yourself out of this jamb? One way would be to apologize to Britain and keep your mouth closed and pay the taxes, or another way would be to possibly bluff your way out of it. Draw up a resolution demanding equal representation and equal taxation.

Now, you have to take into consideration that Britain had already claimed the land for itself by either conning or forcibly taking it from the native population. The point is that Britain felt that they owned it and therefore they felt that they had the right to collect whatever wealth off of it as they saw fit. This is similar to how the United States feels about its property inside of its borders and its "Possessions" outside of its borders as well. "To the victor go the spoils." Now Britain was being questioned by its tenants, "Colonists", about being unfairly taxed and unfairly represented in Parliament.

When you anger someone who is bigger and stronger than you and a fight, or possibly prison time is looming on the horizon, you might better find an ally to help you, stand up with you so to say. The more that will help you the chances are you might prove a point and not get killed or sent to prison in the process.

Since you are the minority, the wealthier and more educated than the majority (the common man who in most cases could not read or write), you need to get them convinced that your cause is a just cause. You could offer them some of your wealth, but you don't have enough and they might get as greedy as you and demand more latter on. Since you don't have anything to offer them for their help, then you must turn your cause into their cause. To do that you need to convince them that their livelihood is in just as much jeopardy as yours.

I have been in many bar rooms, among other places, where gossip and conversations turn a point of view into an accepted point of view, no matter if the point of view is a justifiable true one or not. This happens because the listener is too dumb and drunk to think rationally. For example, how many drunks think rationally enough that they can drive home safely after they get to the point where they have a hard time speaking and walking? It is easy to get a person who is a little drunk to believe in something they know very little if anything at all about. This is another perfect example of the use of "scare tactics".

When you are buying rounds of ale and are telling your listeners that the British are going to tax you to death and their soldiers are going to come and make you do as they want you to and take what you have worked your ass off to acquire, you have their attention. Not just because you're buying them ale, but because you are inserting a thought and playing into their fears. That's where the gossip and rumors come in that you planted into the right ears a month or so before. If you are a little drunk and a little less educated than you should be, and someone is preaching into your fears, you will get all riled up and looking for a fight.

Even today, playing into the ploy of people's fears can rally together a group of people to act out. The Tea Party Effect is a good example of playing into people's fears and getting everyone going out half cocked on a subject without the knowledge of what the problem is actually about. Another good example was why we invaded Iraq. Simply put, scare tactics from a group that has a lot to lose and/or a lot to gain preying on a group who technically do not have all that much to lose and not all that much to gain.

This is basically how the Revolutionary War got rolling along. Even today, we declared war on Iraq because of the thought imposed onto the American People that Iraq had "Weapons of Mass Destruction", which is nothing more than a scare tactic.

This basically is the reason why the American People do not elect their President. A group of people called "Electoral" actually choose the President of the United States. This is all thanks to the "Constitutional Convention of September 7, 1787, where one suggestion was to let the people direct vote for their president. The delegates at this affair decided that the American People were not "mature" enough for this responsibility. Apparently, in their eyes "We the People" are too stupid and too easily influenced to pick the right president to lead us, one that the rest of the government would rather not have. Look how easily we were talked into a revolutionary war.

Now don't get me wrong, we needed to free ourselves from British rule, but "We the People" didn't want to be caught back into the same scenario as we fought to leave. The difference is that instead of having a King and a distant government and its appointed overseers ruling us, we have a President we actually don't directly elect and we have Representatives and Senators we elect, but are put in the position for our votes by the big businesses and all of the money they dump into "those running for office" campaigns through various means.

Even our own Government had acceptance for slavery, and not just blacks were enslaved. Native Americans were the first slaves by Europeans in America. My Grandmother's family was indentured servants. Basically, they were white slaves given passage from Europe and having to work for free until at such point in time where they had earned their freedom.

We are basically offered a choice from two parties, the Democrats and the Republicans. Though there is the Independent and Green Parties, there isn't enough money behind their candidates to make a legitimate run. It basically boils down to who can spend the most money to get elected. Show me a common person running for Congress or the Senate in a very populated area, or even the Presidency and he better have backers with at least a few hundred thousand or a few million to spend or they will go no where fast.

We basically are voting for the lesser of two evils, voting for a candidate that will do the less damage, we hope. In the lesser populated areas there are candidates that are running for an office in a district that really doesn't have enough political clout to make any difference.

In lesser districts where there are not as many constituents that would make any difference on any national matter, a candidate wouldn't need an astronomical amount of money to run for office. This location wouldn't be in the best interests for "big money", unless of course that area had potential for investment.

I live in such a district in Berkshire County of Western Massachusetts. No matter who we elect its like "pissing in the wind" when it comes to having a legitimate say in our state, not to mention nationally. The problem is that if a candidate gets elected in areas like mine, he or she succumbs to the "glitter and glamour" of politics and is usually eaten up by those career politicians that have been there long enough, are wealthy enough, and have had their pockets lined substantially enough by "Big Business", that they make a fool out of those that don't play along. It is like being controlled by the bullies on the playground. It's Human Nature as well as the Law of Survival, "the strongest survive and the weak succumb or perish".

"We the People" don't even get to vote on policies that run our lives. We elect the Congress and the Senate to look out for "our best interests", but all of them received money to campaign with from big corporations and wealthy individuals, the wealth of the nation. So, who do you think they will represent more, the wealthy minority or the poor slobs' majority? Whose ass would you kiss if you were in their shoes? My point made.

Who makes the policies that rule our lives? Senators and Representatives make up the laws that we have to abide by and they usually have law degrees or at least studied law in college. "We the People" are fed a bone from time to time, but on the most part most policies usually benefit the wealthy and the big industries. Who gave the banking industries free reins awhile ago and took away any government control or even overseeing any of their practices, which led to the current financial crisis? Who represents these companies, Lawyers do. Yes, we need the big industries here in this country to help keep our citizens employed, but the government kisses their asses way too much. These companies, such as the oil companies, pay very little taxes and some get initiatives as in tax breaks to keep their companies here in the US. If they wanted to move their industries elsewhere then we could boycott their products. We are the largest group of consumers on this planet and that should give us plenty of clout, you would think.

The reason our government kisses the big industries asses is because there are kick backs to be had for our politicians. If not direct kick backs the big industries supply plenty of funds for election campaigns for the politicians that kiss their asses the most. The last time I remember, bribes were illegal in the United States. Then, why are politicians and lobbyists getting away with it at "We the People's" expense? Eliminate the loopholes and open up the Government to accountability and honesty!

Who gets it up their ass in the end? "We the People" of course, by the high prices we pay for everything in our lives. The prices we pay for energy, such as fuel for our vehicles, electricity and fuel for heating our homes, are controlled by the companies that show huge profits. Does everyone remember Enron and Exxon Mobile and the huge profits they made?

"We the People" should have a say in the laws and policies that rule our lives. There should never be a law passed by this government that directly affects our lives substantially without a direct vote on it from every citizen in this country that chooses to vote on it. There should be no attachments or pork barrel spending allowed on any bill. The American People should be well informed with truth and honesty about any of these bills and not have certain facts about these bills be over exaggerated to make them more or less appealing. Overall the American People are tired of being lied to and we are tired of the scare tactics that we are constantly being bombarded with.

For the average American Citizen to be well informed we need honesty from our government. To help our government to become forthwith and honest, it is the duty of the news media to check the facts our Government spews out. People of a free nation have to rely on the news media, not only the media of this nation but from outside its borders, to be our "News Police" so to say, and help keep our government honest. The News Media have an obligation to report honest facts of all sides. When they don't, then they are no different than our government when it lies to the American People.

Our politicians are acting like juvenile children that live their lives without any restrictions, no authority figure watching them, and no discipline. They were given an inch and they took thousands of miles. If you think that what I propose is absurd and impossible to achieve, if you feel that when we elect members of the House and the Senate that they are supposed to govern on our behalf, and I ask you, why are we in the mess today that we are in with a very severe financial crisis and two wars we are still fighting? So, are we Free?

In my life time I have seen gas prices double and triple in the course of a few short months on three separate occasions. I heard all of the excuses and I wondered who was getting rich on these scams. The oil companies made record profits after each incident. Our government allowed it to go on. Hell, we've had a few oil barons as presidents. Who pays for it in the long run?

I met a man once from Pakistan. He worked for an oil company in the Middle East as an engineer. He told me that it was estimated that the Middle East had enough oil in the ground to last until around 2040.

Then the oil companies of the United States would be able to completely control the price of oil from then on. The technology to eliminate the need for oil has been squashed since the 1950's and who would profit greatly by all of this?

Every time a major meltdown in our economy occurred it can be traced back to our government mishandling it, and they say we the common people are too ignorant to elect a president. Most recently we have been in a very tragic economical down turn to say the least. It didn't happen over night, it took almost a couple of decades of greed in the financial world to build up an excess of new wealth. The internet was booming, some of the common people were creating nice nest eggs for their retirement with the stock market reaching new highs. Americans along with the rest of the world were spending more and more money on more and more luxury items, such as cars and homes. Prosperity looked so good that it was like riding a surf board on a tsunami wave, exciting and fun, a big high, and like the tsunami, it left a path of destruction in its aftermath. Our greed got the better of us all.

Because of the good feeling we all had we began to extend ourselves financially out farther than we could sensibly afford, and there in the plain sight were banks and lending institutions ready to lend us the money without concern, because they would simply sell our loans to another corporation, who would sell to still another corporation, until like the musical chair game, the one left standing got screwed. Then it was "Oh my God", our banks our going to go bankrupt and the world will fall into anarchy, and this government had to bail out the banking industry because the banks made too many bad investments. "The whole world was going to fail." Who let them fail? Who gave them a bail out cash flow with no strings attached? Who gave them the power to do as they please with no restrictions and no over sight? Whenever I applied for a loan the banks made me jump through hoops before I received it.

Did any of the banking executives suffer like us common folk? All of them still received their salaries and received large bonuses. I doubt that they ever worried about where their next meal might come from, or if they could afford to pay the heating bill for the winter. It seems to me that they did this to earn huge profits and the hell with the rest of the population. What they did to the American People was nothing more than a scam. No different than what Enron did. By the way, how many of them do any jail time for scamming the American People?

Yes, the common person should have used some common sense and not over extended their credit, but why did the banking industry allow those individuals to over extend? As I explained before they played musical chairs and those that got caught without a seat when the bubble burst got bailed out by our government with "We the People's" hard earned tax money, plain and simple. Keep this in mind, it took around twenty years for it to build and blow up in our faces, it is going to take some time for the wounds to heal before we get back to a comfort zone we expect to be in before we are comfortable.

Throughout American History during every conquest, the settling of the American West and Alaska, the American Government had no disregards for human rights and respect for other's property. When they purchased from a third party or flat out infiltrated and took from its owners these new frontiers, they basically were doing it the same way as the rest of the world did it, especially Europe. Where do you think they learned it from? Conquest of Kings and Queens, and Emperors, has gone on since the dawn of civilized man. If our intentions for getting away from England and the rest of Europe for that matter, was because we didn't like the way they were doing things, the unfairness of how Britain treated the colonists, then why did we, and are still doing it, the same way as they did it?

Now correct me if I'm wrong but I was taught that forcibly taking or stealing something that someone else owns is against the law. To purchase that item from the person who took it is still against the law. The Conquest of the Americas, the Louisiana Purchase, all seem to fall into this category. Unfortunately, this was the common practice throughout the world back then.

It took a Civil War to abolish slavery. It took almost a century and a half to let a woman have the right to vote and almost two hundred years to allow a person of dark skin to vote as well. It took violence and unions fighting violently back to gain workers' rights and to make the work place safer for workers. Can you tell me who backed all of those big business that were making the huge profits on the backs of all of those people who finally earned their rights that were supposedly granted to them by the Constitution of the United States?

If you look close enough at American History you will see time and time again the abuse of wealth and power over the less fortunate, and this wealth and power will usually be backed by the United States Government.

The Pursuit of Wealth is the given right of the American People, but it should also have been made as part of that law that the wealth should not have been pursued by means of disregard for human rights and that a fair share of that wealth should have been given to those who helped earn it.

Native Americans use to own the Americas. They were unable to defend their lands against the Europeans because of the Europeans' wealth and the power it bought. When the Native Americans surrendered, they were placed on reservations. When there was wealth found on these reservations, Gold, Silver, and Oil, their land was stolen again and they were given even worse land to live on. Genocide was practiced on them by the American Government. The battle of "Wounded Knee" in 1890 and again in 1973, are good examples of how typically this government works in getting what it wants. Another good example is the shooting of four college students at Kent State on May 4th, 1970. This was a message sent to the youth of America that we are not free.

My friend the plumber constantly complains about being hounded for Jury Duty. He has gotten out of it so far, by pleading to the court that he can not honestly force himself to pass judgment onto another person. If he sentenced an innocent person to jail then he couldn't live with the guilt. My friend is telling the truth on this point. Every three years he is pestered for jury duty. He was told that if he refused he could be sent to jail. Does this sound like a free country to you? My friend has stated that when his children are out of school and on their own, he is going to refuse to even answer the Jury Notification. At this point in his life, he is willing to even die for simply standing for what he believes in. I heard him say that if the courts want to turn him into a criminal for simply refusing to take part in Jury Duty, then so be it. If it is a war they want, then it will be a war they will get!

I have another friend who has a wife that is not a citizen of the United States. She in fact is a Registered Alien. She continually receives notices for Jury Duty, and every time they send the form back and state that she is not a citizen and they continually send her Jury Notification. Now tell me, at what point in time will the court system figure out that their system is flawed and will correct it? Again, it is not rocket science. Are there real idiots working there or do they intentionally intend to piss people off enough to actually, in the court's eyes, turn honest, normally law abiding citizens into frustrated and angry criminals?

The way the court systems are run it seems that the more money you have the better off you are. It doesn't matter whether you are guilty or innocent if you have a real snake for a lawyer and they are better than the lawyer for the other side, then you'll get off. Of course, the more money you have the nastier snake of a lawyer you can afford. The problem is that Lawyers wrote the rules that courts go by and they sure as hell left enough loop holes for themselves to save their own asses if they ever needed to. If they didn't then they were pretty stupid not to. So tell me, have you ever known a good lawyer that was that stupid?

"We the People" are still unfairly represented. On the local level is the only place that we are offered more than two candidates to choose from when voting for government officials. As far as our so called State Representatives and Senators, it is between a Republican and a Democrat. Very rarely is an Independent there to run for an office, and he or she is usually just another Democrat or Republican that wasn't chosen to represent their party. Yes there are other sub parties that offer a person, but it's how much you can spend that gets you selected and puts you on the ballot. There should be a reasonable limit to what can be spent on campaigning for any public office. A low enough limit so that a common man can run and have as good of a chance as anyone else.

Too many times I have heard campaign promises made and never fulfilled. There should be a well publicized report card on their goals promised and goals achieved. I can't tell you how much I hate hearing about how bad or how good an elected official was and not knowing how much truth there was in that information. I am tired of all of the lies. For once I wish all public officials would be up front and honest and hold themselves accountable to the people they are supposed to represent. Unfortunately, if a good and honest person was elected they would fall into the trap designed by the government originally to not allow itself to change. It was designed to represent big business and big money foremost. "We the People" are only given a bone once in awhile to settle any uprising we might try.

Case in point, in the sixties and seventies, the youth of this era were organizing with large demonstrations. They demanded the war in Vietnam be halted. They demanded that an Eighteen year old be allowed to vote. They demanded less censorship of public speaking and they wanted their voices to be heard by all. The incident at Kent State where four protestors were shot and killed is a good example of the government trying to put down an uprising with force. When they couldn't stop the youth of America and the rest of the world began to join in, then a couple of bones were offered, and the youth settled down. Eighteen year olds were allowed to vote, the drafting of young men for armed services was ended, and sexual harassment along with domestic violence became legitimately illegal. Then we had the gas shortage of Nineteen Seventy-three and Seventy-four, and that threw fear into everyone and changed the focus from protesting against too much government control to another serious issue.

I learned a long time ago that the average person that lives a fairly decent lifestyle doesn't really care about what goes on in the world. I'm not just talking about the average person in the United States, but everyone in most countries in Europe and around the rest of the world. They may seem to care when they see atrocities on the television and some may even act on it by getting a little involved in changing the situation for the better. As long as the average person in their own opinion has a comfortable life to live, a comfortable home to go to, a job, food on the table, money to buy clothes and some luxury items, if they own a vehicle and they can buy fuel for it, either all of the above or at least most of the above, they really don't want to know about what dirty deals were made behind closed doors to keep their comfortable lifestyle going. When there is an interruption in their comfortable lifestyle, such as the gas shortage of the early Seventies, then the average person will go along with anything that gets their lifestyle back to what they consider normal. Most of the time they don't care what the price is, or even who lives and who dies, and they forget all about what concerns they had previously.

If you looked back through the past two hundred or so years and looked at all of the tragic events that happened around the world, you will find that the people of that country went along with their government's actions just to get back to their comfort zone. Whether or not the government of that country allowed it to happen, or if the people going along with their government's unfair actions were mislead with the wrong information or not, the average person's comfortable lifestyle was threatened and the people could not allow it to get any worse. So, they went along with whatever their government told them as long as their comfort level went back to the way it was before.

One example of this is the way Europe conquered the world and placed settlements all over it. The native people that were conquered were in most cases enslaved or killed, in some cases whole cultures of people were wiped out. It was the thing to do during those times and had been since the dawn of civilized man. The common people of those countries that did the conquering went along with it because they had no choice on the matter to start with, and it could lead to a better lifestyle for them anyway. Whether or not it was for the quest for silver and gold, or for religious freedom, or for land, the common person went along with their rulers' decisions.

When American settlers pushed towards the Mississippi River and beyond, the native people of those areas were almost completely wiped out and were forced into reservations that couldn't sustain their native lifestyle. The average American didn't care. They saw their lifestyle continuing or improving.

When the American Civil War ended, so did slavery, but look how long it took for Black Americans to finally be somewhat equal to a White American. After the war, the average American of the North didn't really care, because their lifestyle would stay the same or improve. The average person of the South lost out and had to struggle to get their lifestyle back to the pre-war comfort, even if it meant to accept the North's new rules.

When Germany conquered Europe and Japan had conquered Pacific Asia, the German and Japanese people would see their lifestyle continuing and they could have a chance to prosper. When both countries were defeated in the end, their people suffered severely as did the countries that they had earlier conquered. The people of the United States, England, and Russia didn't care who suffered. Their countries' governments divided Germany, Korea, Vietnam, half of Europe, and the Middle East amongst themselves. They placed puppet governments into power there and the average person from each of the three countries didn't care. We empowered a Shah in Iran as our puppet.

The people of Britain and the United States would continue their lifestyles and even prosper. In America it would mean cheap oil and the oil industry prospered greatly. What about the countries that were originally conquered and re-conquered again to "liberate", and the people of these countries had to suffer further, did anyone care? No one in America did because their lifestyle was safe.

We recently went to war in Iraq to depose the dictator there. We went there under false pretenses under the supposed fear that Saddam was developing weapons of mass destruction. Let's face it, the American people were tired of hearing about how cruel Saddam was to his own people and about all of the bad things he said about us. When it was stated by our own administration of the time that Saddam was close to developing nuclear weapons, ninety percent of all Americans wanted his head on a platter. We as a nation were ready for a war. We had just gone through the tragedy of the Nine Eleven Attack in New York City, we were ready to invade Afghanistan, and we as Americans were afraid that our comfortable lifestyle was being threatened. We didn't care what dirty deal was being made behind any closed door and we didn't care who would live or who would die.

Yes, hind sight is wonderful, but the point of the matter is we were lied to, no one was ever held accountable for the lies, and our government will continue doing business without our approval because that is the way it is designed to operate. It was not designed to be governed by "We the People" it was designed to be governed by big wealth and big business. That is were the power is and as long as the average American has a comfortable lifestyle we don't care, and whenever we start to get out of line and too "uppity" then the government throws a tragedy at us and threatens our comfort zone, and we back down in fear. So tell me, Are We Free?

Do you ever wonder why we as Americans are hated around the world? Two things you need to look at, and I know all about this because I have been around the world a few times and have seen it with my own and opened eyes. First of all, Americans have a tendency to act like their "shit doesn't stink" while in other countries. They forget that they are guests in that country and they should be humble and respective to their hosts. Secondly, if a country has a natural resource that any American company can go in and take advantage of and make huge profits from, they will do so. They will even take advantage of the people of that country, far worse than they would take advantage of the American people because they can get away with it in certain countries. If another country came to America and made a deal with our government to take our natural resources from us and we as average Americans would see our comfortable lifestyles diminish along with our natural resources, we would be pretty well pissed at that country's government and its people as well. Wouldn't you agree?

Japan in the 1970's and 1980's had become a world power and were buying up our real-estate on our home turf. They formed big businesses and the American People felt threatened. There were many that began to hate the Japanese and their big businesses. Does this sound familiar? The Japanese people were being treated in the United States like we are treated around the world.

The Middle East is known for its abundance of crude oil. After World War Two the United States and England had "acquired" the rights to that oil at the expense of those countries' people. "To the victor go the spoils." Some of those countries' leaders made huge profits on these deals, as well as the oil companies of the United States and England. For those countries in the Middle East that didn't have ruling Royal Families, we placed someone in that leadership role who would give our oil companies a free hand to do as they please. The average person of the Middle East saw their natural resources leaving their countries and they were not seeing their way of life getting any better. In some cases it even got worse.

After World War One Britain and the League of Nations allowed Palestine to become more occupied by emigrating Jewish People, who were hoping to create a Jewish State in their original homeland. During and after World War Two the United States got involved because of Jewish influence in the government at home.

By the time Israel had become a nation, most of the Palestinians had been pushed out of Palestine and had to live in surrounding countries, which those surrounding countries in turn didn't like what was going on and despised the Jews for doing this to the Palestinians. Eventually, the American People were looked at as aiding culprits to this whole affair. Because our government usually goes along and allows Israel to do as they want, we as a people are hated in the Middle East.

Terrorism was used by both the Israelis and the Palestinians against each other during their early conflicts in the late Nineteen Forties. When you add in the fact that the money flow from Jews in Europe and America was used for the purchase of weapons for the Israelis, and the United Nations giving the Israelis the right to recognize Israel as a legitimate nation, it's a wonder there wasn't a war against our businesses operating in the Middle East. Eventually we were booted out of Iran and Iraq, and other Middle Eastern countries as well.

The Middle East has always been a hot spot for war because of its location and now for its oil. They have something the world wants and the world has been taking what it wants for decades and the common people of those lands our going through what we did during our revolutionary times.

So, you see why we are hated throughout the world, just like we despised English rule and its soldiers. We have the tendency to stick our noses in places where they don't really belong and all for the quest of wealth and power.

Do we have a government that's too big? When a government is so big that it has Agencies and Departments kept secret from its own people, when it walks hand in hand with wealthy "Big Businesses", it is never held accountable for its actions, when taxes are collected and spent in ways that the common person is never told about nor has any control over, when our government supplies groups of people to secretly fight our so called enemies and then those we supported turn on us, when "We The People" don't really have a say in what laws and policies are passed, yea, it's too damn big.

I continually hear the comments about the fear of the United States turning Socialistic. I've got news for you. You are hiding your eyes and ears from the world around you. I really do not see all that much difference now. With eyes wide open I have looked back on history, I have looked back on the evolution of war, I have studied psychology to a point, I know what "scare tactics" are and how they are used effectively, and I don't see grounds for your point of view. You have fallen into their trap with eyes closed and faith to the wind, head up your ass, and a very naïve outlook of your life in general!

There are those who fear government controlled health care, regulations on the banking industry, gun control, freedom of speech, and the likes. They fear that the government is getting too big and it will lead to a partial Socialistic State. Let us compare Socialism and Capitalism.

In Socialistic, or Communistic Societies, like Russia and China, there is a majority of middle class people as well as a substantial lower class. These classes make up the work force. The same goes for Capitalistic Societies as well, like the United States and Great Britain. In Socialism you have a government run health care system for all. In Capitalism Individuals have to pay for health care, which is why there are a substantial amount of individuals who are not covered under a health care plan and are usually under some form of a government assisted plan, "Welfare", Medicaid", or they simply have to much pride to accept any form of a handout and have no health insurance.

In Socialism the government is appointed by the main body of self appointed leaders. They rule the country and they control the wealth of the country as well. In a Capitalistic society like the United States, the people pick their local representatives out of a small list of candidates who want to run for that office. When they elect their State Representatives, the Senate and the Congress, they first select in a pre election from a small list of candidates for each of the two parties. When one is selected to represent each party, then the people of that state elect one of those to represent them in their own state and also in Washington, but we don't elect the President.

We all know our Government keeps an awful lot of secrets from "We the People" and there is nothing we can do about it. Some of these secrets may be a legitimate reason for National Security, but there is an awful lot that isn't. We also know that our Government passes bills that become a part of our laws that the majority of "We the People" don't agree with. Any information about these bills that are passed is sometimes very much impossible to understand. Usually they contain "Pork" or little "add on parts" that add more money to these bills that we have to fork out to pay for and most of the time these add on parts are nothing more than crap that puts money in someone's pocket that is looking for a "kick back" from the Senator or Congressman that put the "pork" in the bill to start with.

So, do we have control of our Government or are we <u>No Different</u> than a Socialistic Government? Yes, we have a "Little Say" in what goes on, but "We the Common People" are left out of the loop, so to say, when it involves the "Bottom Line" for Big Businesses, when it comes to what is done in our Government.

As I stated before, the more money the candidate has to spend for campaigning the likelihood he or she will get elected. The same goes as for the president, except as stated before "We the People" really don't elect them either. The majority of the wealth is controlled by big businesses, which in turn influences the decisions our government officials make. Now these elected officials are supposed to represent our best interests, but be honest, how often do any of them really. It sort of looks like big businesses are acting like self appointed leaders in a Socialistic State and they place in office the "Puppet Politicians" they want there on their behalf. Remember my comment before about "Wealth is Power and Power is Wealth"?

Here in Western Massachusetts the eastern end of the state spent a considerable few billions of dollars in a project called the "Big Dig", and it had considerable amounts of job cost overruns as well. It basically was a rebuild of the roads and highways in Boston to help with traffic problems there. I know that during that time period and after that, here in the western part of the state, our roads really sucked. Very little money was funneled our way to do a half assed repair, but we helped foot the bill for the Big Dig and the vast majority of us in the western end will never use it. It didn't look to me like we were well represented. Again, the politicians in our area were succumbed to the glitter and glamour of the big influential politicians of the more populated and more financially influenced Eastern end. I'm sure that you can come up with a similar story as well in your state.

Now, looking at the Gun Control issue, in Socialism no one but the military are allowed to own guns except in very rural parts for hunting purposes only. In Capitalism our second amendment states that "we have the right to bear arms to support a militia to secure the right to maintain a free state". There are many in Washington that fear that and are trying to take our guns away.

In Socialism the people are very limited to what they say about their government. In Capitalism we were given the right for freedom of speech, but ask those in the Sixties and early Seventies involved in the peace movement about the freedom of speech, especially the four who died at Kent State. Asked those blacks that marched on the streets in the Sixties about how hard it was to earn their rights of equality. Ask those who were accused of believing in the Communist Movement in the United States during the McCarthy Era and those in the entertaining industry who were black listed for it, about the right for the Freedom of Speech. Ask those who died at Wounded Knee during both events about the right for the Freedom of Speech.

If I have upset anyone with my opinion, then I apologize, but I have not said anything that is not the truth. My father and I had many of arguments on the matter of being free and living in this country. He believed in the "Bullshit" that was preached and I don't. If this country was truly free for "We the People" then "Big Business" wouldn't control our Governmental Leaders that "We the People" supposedly picked, and "We the People" would have the final say on what Bills of Government are passed and what are not, and we would have a better choice of who we elect to represent Us as a People, and we would not be lied to, kept secrets from, and would be given complete control of a Government that was supposed to be "For the People, By the People, Of the People".

I did my time for the government and I've heard the comments from soldiers who fought in World War Two, in 'Nam, and in the Iraqi and Afghanistan wars, about fighting in combat for the freedoms here at home. Comments like, "I didn't fight over there to defend our freedoms to listen to their crap!" These comments were made in reference to those who spoke out against the wars in 'Nam and the Middle East. My father made many such comments whenever he saw the news in the Sixties reporting on the Peace Movement and young men who were burning their draft cards and running to Canada to avoid the draft.

Our soldiers fought in wars that not always were for defending our rights for freedom. Nor did we necessarily fight for the rights and freedom of those countries we were defending. When we are at war where there is a threat to our freedoms, our soldiers are fighting for those exact freedoms that protestors against a war are exercising, the Freedom of Speech". Protestors need to understand that a soldier follows orders. Do not blame them for this. A soldier is trained primarily to kill. It is not a pretty thought but it is a fact of life. Sometimes a life or death decision is made in a fraction of a second. A soldier has to live with that decision for the rest of their life. A soldier sees ten times the things he will ever see in his life, and sometimes it ruins a soldier's life. Not every soldier is a natural born soldier. It is very hard to see death and not let it bother you, no matter whose death it is. I am not stating that our soldiers are perfect and they can do no wrong. Sometimes a soldier can get carried away and do the wrong thing, above and beyond the call of duty. Then, and only then should they be held accountable for their actions, including officers, because, what's fair is fair.

By the same flip of a coin, soldiers should not condemn protestors for doing so. Not every war was fought for the protection of our freedoms. Vietnam and Korea should never have been split up as a compromise between Communism and Capitalism, spoils of war. The Vietnamese and Korean people should have had the right themselves to choose between Communism and Capitalism, not the United States, Britain, and the USSR!

Far too many of the wars were fought for the rights of big businesses and big industries to be able to go into a country to pillage its resources. If you don't believe me, then think about who had the most to gain by the war. Then think about why it took so long for the United States to get involved in the Bosnian Conflict, and why we never helped out any country in Africa with solid force that is going through a civil war with genocide being practiced by the stronger armed forces of those areas. Why did it take a Japanese Invasion on Pearl Harbor to get us physically involved with the fighting in Europe? It was because our big businesses were making hand over fist big profits supplying food, weapons, machinery to most of the countries already involved in the war.

A soldier is trained to follow orders and never to question them. It is a necessity to have them do this because in battle, <u>A Soldier Can Not Hesitate</u>. Their life and those around them depend on it. If "We the People" had more of a choice in which wars we should fight, and we had more of a say in our policies around the world, then our soldiers would be fighting for a just cause and not to protect the wealth of Big Businesses around the world. How many of our soldiers come home after serving our country in combat and can't adjust back to civilian life? How many soldiers come back physically scarred and handicapped for life and our government turns its back on them? As far as I'm concerned, if a soldier puts their life on the line for our soil, our way of life, our people, and our government, the Government better damn well take good care of them physically, mentally, emotionally, and financially. They sure as hell deserved it!

As far as speaking your mind, mention the wrong words too often over the phone or over the internet and then keep a close eye on what vehicles are following you for the next two or three weeks. I have a friend that use to work for the government. He does this occasionally to let the government know that not only does he know that they are watching him, that also he is watching them.

There are some differences in Socialism and Capitalism as well as a lot of similarities. We in the United States have come a long ways from our earlier times. We are not perfect. We are still an arrogant group of people. We stick our noses in places we shouldn't and we don't in places we should, it all depends on if there is a profit in it or not. Let's face it, the only reason we went to war in Iraq was to secure the oil rights for our big business oil companies. We don't help the innocent people that are being massacred in places like Sierra Leone, Somalia, and Ethiopia among others because they have nothing of wealth to offer. They have no strategic area that would help in our national defense, like seaports, landing fields, or radar positioning.

So, I ask again, are we as free as you think?

- We don't directly vote for our President
- We aren't given a good choice for voting for who represents us. We need to get rid of the two party system and place low enough limits for campaigning so good and honest people can run for office and represent us properly, and stop voting for the lesser of two evils
- Speak the wrong words and you could end up being interrogated or beaten by an angry mob, or by one of the many secret government agencies we no nothing about
- You have the right to own guns and ammunition but some of us have to jump through hoops to purchase them while criminals don't. Gun laws should be a National Law, not and Individual State Law
- You have the right to pursue wealth, but a common person becoming wealthy has the same odds as hitting the lottery. It seems as though every time the economy is doing well and people are earning decent money and spending some of it along the way and boosting the economy, there is always something that happens to the economy to take that away from us; the current banking and housing collapse, oil prices jumping up from time to time. The rich will get richer and the poor will always be poor

So, we are not that much different than a Socialistic Government and I am tired of anyone out there that wants to Preach to me that we are so "God Damn Free" that if I don't like it then I can leave. So much for the freedom of speech. Those who believe this are no better than the Dictators of Socialistic Countries. They are no different than the Ku Klux Klan. They are no different than those that believe that their God is the only one and anyone who doesn't agree can burn in hell. All of those people that are so one sided and closed minded are seriously no different than those that run a Socialistic State. This country was supposed to be based on Freedom of Religion and Freedom of Speech, yet the typical American Citizen is no different than a sheep in a flock that needs a Sheppard to herd them, a Sheppard that represents a Government that controls its people, telling us to vote for the lesser of two evils, taking our hard earned money and not giving us a full and truthful account of where it is being spent. So, Are We Free?

What are "Scare Tactics" you might be asking? Remember when your parents told you when you were little that if you go out in the cold without a jacket you are going to catch a cold? Be careful with that, you could poke someone's eye out with it! Have you ever been forced to buy something because you were told that the price of the item was going to increase considerably, and a short time later it actually was cheaper? When was the last time you needed something repaired and the repair person talked you into buying a new item to replace the old one when there was nothing really badly wrong with the old one to start with? Have you ever been told that if you don't believe in their God and repent and confess your sins that you will die and go to hell? A "Scare Tactic" is when someone uses fear in the unknown to get you to do as they wish.

Search your memories and I'm sure you have been a victim a few times in your life. The Iraqi war was one big "Scare Tactic" to get the American People to go along with it. We were told that Iraq was developing "Weapons of Mass Destruction" and "al-Qaeda had training camps there, and the time was now to invade and take away the threat! Did they find this "Solid Proof" of a threat? Now it seems that the sure mention of 911 and everyone trembles in their shoes and the government again will be allowed to do as they please. Sounds more and more like scare tactics to keep a nation of people in check and obedient when they are questioning their leaders.

What do the Democrats and Republicans stand for? To be honest I'm as confused as you are. It used to be that the Republicans represented the common man and the Democrats represented Big Businesses. That was when the common man was really getting shit upon. We had slavery, very low wages, white males were only allowed to vote. Sometime after the turn of the century it reversed. Now, it looks to me to be a free for all and "We the People" are still getting it shoved down our throats. Both parties kiss Big Businesses' ass so they can get re-elected. Now we have high unemployment, crappy healthcare law shoved down our throats with our own money paying for it in the long run, drugs on the streets, and oil companies excitedly waiting to jack the price of oil up again, our borders being laughed at by the world, and banks and financial institutions falling into the manure pile and coming out smelling like a rose.

Out of the pockets of "We the People" the failing banks were given billions and billions of dollars to bail them out, with NO STRINGS ATTACHED, because of very irresponsible dealings on their part and our Government's as well. How stupid is that. Now I ask, did anyone that was employed by these banks and financial institutions that received this bail out money, and I'm pointing at those that earned at least two hundred thousand dollars or more, had to worry if they were going to lose their home or wonder where their next meal would come from?

Their selfish and irresponsible acts caused most, if not all of the financial woes that "We the People" are suffering now. Has anyone been held completely accountable? Between the executives of all of these banks, right down to their employees that helped make the decisions to cause these problems, to the politicians who gave them free reins to do as they please, no one was ever held accountable. They all collected their salaries without any disruptions. If any one of us, "We the Common People" ever did anything like that, we would be doing prison time. What the Financial Institutions did was no different than if I went into your home and stole every one of your possessions, including your own home, right out from under you. Now tell me the truth on this thought. Did "We the People" have the final say on how to solve this problem? Were we allowed to hold completely accountable all those that were involved, and I would include all of the Politicians that voted to bail out the banks with no strings attached? Not by a long shot! Sure sounds like one big scam to me!

Our own government officials are pitting the American People against each other with their lies and deceptions and the stretching of the truths. Where in hell is the accountability that each and every one of us should be exercising, especially in these troubled times? And you tell me we are free? Bullshit!!!

When the Declaration of Independence was drafted, signed, and sent to England, "We the People" was written boldly on it, but it didn't truly represent "All of We the People". It couldn't have when there was slavery existing, women were treated as second class citizens, Native Americans were being treated as slaves or even treated as vermin, and the poor uneducated majority that represented the work force were conned into this whole fiasco.

So, in retrospect the American People:

1. Should directly elect their President
2. Have a fare, honest, and better system to elect our public officials, eliminating the two party system, and setting low enough campaigning limits so any intelligent and responsible person can run for any office except the Presidency, which should require fairly good amount of experience in domestic and foreign affairs, and all public officials should be held completely <u>accountable</u> to "All of the People"
3. Will not allow any major legislation to pass <u>without</u> the direct vote of the American People
4. Will be presented for review all legislation to be voted on with "whole truthful facts" without any exaggerations either way of the pros and cons, and in a language that ALL can understand
5. Will not allow any form of "Lobbying" to go on in any form in our Government with our Government Officials and their families and staffs.
6. Will no longer be Spied Upon, Treated as Second Class Citizens, Lied To Anymore, nor Kept From the Truth of what our Government is doing at home and abroad, and if any of this does happen, then "We the People" have a say of the punishment

What Our Government Should Be Like

IN RETROSPECT IT would be great if our Government was "For the People, By the People, Of the People", but it wasn't conceived for that purpose. It was conceived as an illusion of that to serve the purpose of helping big businesses of the times, to acquiring wealth. It fueled the push westward and it has fueled pretty much every war that we were ever involved with.

I have heard the excuses stating that without "Big Business" the common person wouldn't have a job. Our recent and all other recessions prove that point, but there is a limit to how much greed a common person can tolerate. At some point ALL Empires crumble and fall and the common person has their day. It is not the common person that fears having nothing, but rather the wealthy person having to make do with very little. That is and always will be the issue.

When a recession falls upon us the common person is fed the fear of losing everything, and they all buy into the fear. This is nothing but propaganda or scare tactics to get the masses under control. If you think about it, it wouldn't take all that much to throw the world powers on their rears. All it would take is every common person to say that they have had enough, band completely together and help each other, and refuse to work and pay anymore taxes, not to cater to the wealthy, hold fast and make do with very little for as long as it would take, and the world would shut down. The meek would inherit the world. There I go again, day dreaming. It sure would be nice.

On the thought that there wouldn't be any jobs without big business, without small businesses we would be living under a dictatorship. It could be conceived that more people are employed by small businesses than in large conglomerates, and when small businesses are struggling then the common person is struggling as well.

Our Place as Americans around the World is something that I am not proud of. An average American is a greedy and selfish person and we owe it all to the Europeans for giving us this heritage and fueling the fire, so to speak. As I have stated again and again, that when we are in other countries, whether on business or for pleasure, we run around acting like we own the place instead of being humble around our hosts and showing respect. We are always looking for an opportunity to make a buck without the concerns for the aftermath of our actions. It is as if our motto is "Do onto others before they do onto you", but it was never right to do so in the past and it should never be the right way of doing things in the future.

There should never be a starving mother and child, and there should always be enough work for all to earn the right to eat. My Grandfather, my father's father, once told me that you should never forget where you came from, because you may have to go back there someday. Your background that is your personal history is what made you what you are today. Sometimes you need to remember that. Along your journey in life there were those who helped you along the way. Maybe it is time to go back and help them and remember what it was like back then.

Back in the Sixties and early Seventies I have from time to time heard someone tell an African-American that if they didn't like the way things were that they should go back to Africa, even though that person was born here in America. I've heard it said of the Hispanics to go back to Mexico, even though they were from Guatemala or from another Central or South American country. I even heard it said to Native Americans, unfortunately they can't leave and go back to the reservation. This land is their home, so therefore, they are already home.

Home for me is the area where I grew up and stayed to live. Though I could almost live anywhere, I made my choice. When my oldest was in High School and was studying the differences between Capitalism and Socialism, he asked me about the differences between Socialism and Communism. I explained to him that even though most people that live in a Capitalistic Country believe that Socialism and Communism are one in the same, they are different. He asked me if I thought if Communism was better and I explained to him that although it would be better than living in a Socialistic Country, there is still the potential for its leaders to take complete control and turn it into a Socialistic Society. The best solution would be is the best of all worlds. The People would elect those among them to represent them in a Government that was really "For the People, By the People, Of the People". There should be a direct vote from the people of the United States for any major bill where it would affect considerably the life and welfare of the American People.

The President should have goals set from his campaign and be allowed to reach these goals, but it should be the Congress and Senate to look out for the welfare of all of the people and not the wealthy few and the big businesses. A President is elected on the principles of his goals for our country and its people. The Congress and Senate are elected to represent the people of their districts. They should start doing their jobs!

All public officials would be held accountable for their actions. The Congress and the Senate should not get paid if they can't come up with a plan that is fair to all of the people. Any other type of job where you don't perform to the standards your job description outlines you are let go and someone else will take your place. The government is far too big and needs to down size. Very few work a full week, 48 weeks a year, and shouldn't be receiving their pay if they are out campaigning for re-election or running for another office. When a law is being drafted or conceived it should be written in a language that the common person can understand, not a ton of words that explain something that a few words can successfully achieve.

It would be forbidden for any public official to ever tell a lie to the American People or take any form of a bribe, with a punishment of forced resignation and a loss of any benefits including any retirement compensation for such crime. Any Lobbyists caught handing out any form of a bribe to any of our elected officials, including their staffs and their families should face hard prison time.

In a perfect world there would be no need to accumulate wealth. We all would work hard at the job we were most suited for and as we got older and if we worked to our full potential, then we would live a little better, a little easier as we start to approach the end of our life. As our politicians are held accountable, so are each and every individual. If we as the human specie worked together and not against each other, we could take care of our planet, take care of ourselves, not allow hunger, not allow crime, and not allow hate to destroy us. There I go again dreaming.

The Healthcare Issue

I KNOW WHAT its like to have health insurance, and not having any. If you have it through your place of employment it can cost you up to $100.00 per week for a modest plan, including preventive dental and possibly an eye glasses plan. Most plans of this nature have co-pay of $10.00 to $20.00 for each visit, similar co-pay for prescription, and a deductible on hospital visits and stays. At around $100.00 a week through an employer, that's around $5,200.00 a year a family can spend on work place supplied health insurance. That's a third to half the cost of a new car or a nice addition to a down payment to a new house.

Actually, what is Insurance anyway? Well, it's basically a legal form of gambling. You're gambling that something tragic is going to happen to you or one of your loved ones, and the Insurance Companies are gambling that nothing will happen at all, or at least very little. You could safely bet that they will win a high percentage of the time. The few times they do lose, it doesn't really cut all that much into their profits. In the end, if you win, you actually lose. It's a win-win situation for them and a win/lose for you.

When I was a young and single man, and a couple of times while married, I found myself either unemployed or changing jobs and working for another company, and I didn't have any health insurance. Most Doctors and some clinics will give you a good break in fees that they charge if you tell them up front that you are uninsured. Considering at the time I was living on very limited funds, with the few trips to the Doctor's Office I had to make, I actually had put money back into my pocket. I figured I was spending at the time before the job change around $50.00 a week for Health Insurance through work for me and my family. I had to wait six and a half months for the Health Insurance benefit to kick in from the new place of employment. In that time frame I had spent less than a hundred dollars for a couple of office visits and I saved over a thousand dollars.

By law in Massachusetts, when an employee is dismissed or has left the company, they have to be offered Health Insurance under a Cobra Plan. The one that was offered to me cost almost a thousand dollars a month. When you are not working you can't afford it. Also in Massachusetts, the State Government made it against the law to NOT have Health Insurance, and they will fine you when you file your State Income Tax. There is nothing like cramming something down your throat and up your ass the same time.

The average person always has in the back of their mind, "What if something tragically happens to me"? "Can I afford to take the chance?" That's something only you can decide on and no one else can make that decision for you. If you have a family, then it's a decision that the family has to make as a group, or as responsible parents.

Like the political system, there will be Insurance Company Lobbyists pressuring you to get the insurance, through advertisements and TV and radio commercials, and in the shows that are about Hospitals and Emergency Rooms. They will show trauma and people getting injured and getting severely sick and needing expensive care, making you believe you're in danger.

Like the majority of Tobacco financed movies and television shows where the actors and celebrities were shown smoking. "Monkey See, Monkey Do". Though I never smoked cigarettes, but tried a pipe a couple of times, my parents did smoke. Whenever I see someone inhaling a cigarette in a movie or on television, I find myself inhaling. Visual Suggestion is a powerful tool. Even Pharmaceutical Companies with their advertisements for their products are pressuring you to badly need Health Insurance. Television shows about ER's and Hospitals add to your thoughts that something medically will happen to you and your loved ones. You are subconsciously made to believe it is inevitable.

We have to face it. As Humans, we are basically "Scared Sheep" relying on our trusted Sheppard's wisdom for protection, and there are always Wolves among them waiting to take advantage of the poor defenseless sheep. An average person of the United States works hard for the few comforts they can afford. We look at the wealthy and wonder why we aren't as fortunate, and we look at the less fortunate and are glad we are doing better. It is typical Human Behavior no matter what level of income you earn.

To look at the Healthcare Issue this country seems to be in an upheaval over, you need only to break it down to its simplest form of what we actually need. This is the basics for coverage, though there are more details that need to be added and there are much better plans to consider as well, but for now we are only considering what the average person is looking for in what is to be covered under a Health Plan.

- Regular Preventive Check ups—keeps a patient healthy. Like Preventive Dentistry. I go every 6 months and have Not had a cavity in over thirty years. Regular check ups should lessen the un-needed Emergency Room Visits as well.
- Emergency Room Visits—You hope you don't have to use it, but sometimes crap happens. Should be a penalty for frequent use and a savings pay back if not used at all.
- In case of severe illness or extended hospital stay—Everyone would like to live a ripe old age and die healthy, wealthy, and wise, but it seldom works out that way. There should be "Reasonable" deductible and possibly high limits according to levels of coverage. In the rare cases where an expensive treatment or operation is needed to save the life of a child, then that needs to be covered! If it means an "Insurance Pool" of sorts where the very wealthy, the Insurance Companies, Doctors, and Hospitals contribute to it, then make it happen. If a certain procedure is needed to find what is causing a problem, and is a more reliable one than using a cheaper one, if it saves a surgeon from going in blind, then it should be covered. Sometimes X-rays do not show enough detail over an MRI. I've been there and done that and have suffered because of it.
- Pre-existing Condition—Ask a Doctor and they will tell you that the longer you wait to get something medically wrong fixed, the more stress you put onto the rest of your body. This translates into more medical problems. Health Care has to start somewhere. It should have a beginning, when you are

born and an end when you die, hopefully not tragically. A Pre-Existing Condition should not be a reason for denial of coverage. For all of the Pre-existing Conditions that would be imposed on an Insurance Company from new customers, there will be the same amount of customers that an Insurance Company will be passing on to another Insurance Company. It will equal out in the end.

This I believe is the basics, though there are more intricate parts to the coverage. The next thing to consider is that not everyone is on the same pay level. A person or a couple makes a given amount of money a year. Out of that amount come basic living expenses such as housing, food, clothing, utilities, mobility, these are the basics to survive. There is a safe percentage allowance for each of these items that you deduct from your monthly or yearly wage. Included in this formula should be a consideration for health care expense. The rest that's left over is spending money. If a set realistic standard for these percentages was used to base what you should be paying for these necessities, including healthcare, then a person or couple, or family would be obligated to pay that amount.

Now to be fare to all parties involved, there should be 3, 4, 5, or even more levels of coverage to cover the vast spread of yearly salaries that everyone in this country earns. The higher the income the better the coverage, and the higher the percentage a person should be paying, and the differences in percentages should balance out some of the costs for the Insurance Companies. The more you earn the better the coverage you can afford and the higher the percentage allotted from income should be set. This is not to say that you have to accept the better coverage plan if you don't want to.

The wealthier you are the more you contribute to the lower income level's healthcare costs. For each level of income earned there is dependency on all of the other levels. Every level depends on the one basic need that money has to be spent in all levels for any jobs to exist. Without anyone working all of these jobs, no one earns any money. Basically, if the upper levels of income don't want to work the jobs that lower income levels do, then they owe it to pay a little more for Health Care to help offset the costs of the lower levels. When someone is sick or injured and can't perform their job to within the limits of performing that job safely and correctly, then they shouldn't be at work, rather being home and getting better. When someone goes to work sick, then they spread their disease amongst their fellow workers. I've tried to work sick and can not do the job as well as I could have if I were well.

Healthcare Insurance should also penalize with added costs for those covered who don't meet certain criteria. It should also give us a break on costs when we do meet those criteria. It would cut down on obesity, on drug and alcohol related illnesses, and as well as tobacco related illnesses. It would promote exercise and healthy eating habits.

In the end, since the government is making it mandatory for all citizens of the United States to have Healthcare Insurance, then the Insurance Companies Have to be Limited on their profits as well. Just like the Utility Companies are limited. If it is a mandatory necessity, then a high profit should not be allowed to those companies supplying it.

In considering we as Americans are being forced to accept this Healthcare Insurance Policy, no matter what the coverage is, Doctors, Pharmaceutical Companies, the wealthier hospitals, and all other companies and individuals who make a very wealthy living off of the healthcare system should be taking a cut in pay as well to help pay for Healthcare Coverage for all. "What?" you say. "This is not fare to those who have spent their time and money to get into a profession that allows them to make good money and have the responsibility of someone's life in their hands." Without patients neither Doctors nor Hospitals would be needed.

I have a close friend who is a plumber. I've heard him tell a story from time to time about an argument he had with a Doctor, while my friend was working for a big plumbing company. The Doctor was complaining that the plumbing bill was outrageously high and that plumbers in general were over paid. My friend pointed out the fact that he has as much responsibility as the good doctor has, in keeping a family safe, not to mention a community as well. If my friend didn't know what he was doing when it came to piping sewer and sewer vents, installing gas and oil appliances, the fuel piping as well as the venting, potable water connections to non potable water connections, then he could severely injure or even kill a household of people, or even a community. Non potable water is NON Drinkable and a poison and if it got into the water distribution system of a house, public water mains, or even a well, it wouldn't be good.

Water that is in a sewer line, as well as the water in your boiler heating system is non potable water.

If a fuel line to a heating appliance, boilers, furnaces, water heaters, was incorrectly installed and leaked, an explosion could occur. If the exhaust vent of same appliances were not vented correctly, a home could fill with deadly carbon monoxide. Even a garden hose with an insecticide spray container attached to the end of it and connected to the outside faucet, is a potential disaster if a simple little part is not in place on that outside faucet.

So, my friend stated that comparing his pay scale to the good Doctor's, and the similar responsibilities of public safety, my friend should be paid more than what he currently was making. In the end the good Doctor agreed about the responsibilities, but not the pay raise.

Yes, I know it should not be left up to the government to come up with percentages of costs or what is covered and what is not, nor should it be left up to the Insurance Companies. It should be a combination of certain members of the government, Insurance Companies, Doctors, Hospitals, and even a big say from us common folk. We are not as ignorant as we are made to believe.

Do we need Healthcare Insurance? It's a nice idea, but only if it doesn't put us as a Nation too far in debt that our grandchildren won't see the end of the tunnel. As far as the complaints that are out there, that if we impose a government option to be competitive with the insurance companies, it's not a bad idea. As long as the Government can run it efficiently and a lot better than they run the rest of the government, then there shouldn't be any complaints. Will it start to turn us into a Government Controlled State and a step towards Socialism? For those who believe this, let me point it out that we are not as free as you want to believe. Open your eyes and look around you. Walk out of your sheltered lives and stop acting like a flock of sheep and see the whole world, not just the tourist traps. But, that's another issue I'm planning to discuss in the near future.

If Healthcare is being made mandatory for every person in the United States, then it has to be regulated strictly. If it's being crammed down our throats then we should only have to pay a certain percentage of our weekly wages to pay for it. It shouldn't be complicated to use and it better be hassle free. Insurance Companies providing the coverage shouldn't make huge profits on us, Doctors should take a cut in pay to help pay for it, Hospitals shouldn't be making large profits on it to help pay for it, all in all it is feasible to accomplish but it has to be strictly regulated and for all of those that break the rules there should be severe penalties.

Since we are on the Healthcare subject, I have a little note to follow through with. Now I don't want anyone to get too overly offended by my suggestions, but there is a point to where both sides are getting too greedy. Its very similar to when a sports franchise, like the NFL and the NBA when the players go on strike. The league owners are making a bundle on the games and the players want a good portion of it. I have an idea, give half of that profit back to the fans, back to the communities. They deserve it more than any of you do. Without the fans, you would be nothing more than a wanna be.

What this has to do with Healthcare is basically this. Towns, Cities, States, and the Federal Government hire people to perform certain tasks; Teachers, Fireman, Law Enforcement, Office Staff, Janitors, whatever, and they all belong to some form of a Union which negotiates a contract which usually includes a Healthcare Package of some sorts and some form of a retirement package as well.

Now that the "Shit has hit the fan" so to say, with the bad recession we are in, these "Packages" have made it extremely difficult for Towns, Cities, States, and the Federal Government to make ends meet. In some cases it is like the sport franchises, in that both sides are too greedy and should give something back to the tax payers. You pressed for the "Cadillac" of packages when your "Collective Bargaining" forced the Towns, Cities, States, and Federal Government to take the deal or else. Now you are in the same boat as the Auto Workers, and are facing layoffs or cuts to your "Cadillac Packages". Why should you get premium deals when the rest of us get crap? Now the rest of us have to pay for your greed.

I am not just talking to those Unions, I'm also talking to those Towns, Cities, States, and the Federal Government as well. You are in charge of our hard earned tax money we paid in to keep things running smooth. What the hell are we getting for our buck anyway, certainly no accountability anywhere. I personally believe that too many people in these areas are paid way too much for what they are accomplishing. Again, Everyone needs to stop being Greedy! End of conversation!

Religion

I WAS RAISED a Christian and went to Sunday school when I was young. I believed in the thought that Jesus Christ was as great as God. I believed that there was an after life and a Heaven and Hell. In my life I have seen children born and old people die, and accepted the fact that it was apart of the religion that I grew up with and it was a part of life. It was God's will.

I read in history books that we fought our wars with God's blessings, we swore on the Christian Bible "to tell the truth, the whole truth, and nothing but the truth so help me God", and I saw on the currency of the United States that "In God We Trust". When my children were born I had them baptized as Christians.

When I wasn't a teenager anymore I saw what the horrors of war brought. I watched on the television as the news told of genocide being conducted in impoverished nations in Africa, Europe, and Asia. Women and children were raped, killed, and even used as slaves or sold in slavery as well. Yes, even our own soldiers kept a woman or two as a sex slave, with promises of bringing them back as their wives to the "Good Ole US of A", but very seldom ever meaning to do so. Not all soldiers did this, but there were many.

I watched the reporting of people starving to death and dying of deadly diseases. I visited once a children's hospital with a friend to see her daughter who was there with a cancerous tumor in her brain, and I saw all of the children that were there and I wondered what kind of a God would allow this. I've shed too many tears over human suffering that should have never happened and I wondered what kind of an evil species had we become? Later on I looked into my children's eyes and wondered what kind of a father was I to have brought them into such an unjust, unrelenting, and awful world.

I remembered what a close friend had said to me about human nature. That for every two or three steps forward we, as a civilized species takes in our quest to be perfect, we always take a step back because of our animal instincts. This is something that we can never shed. We still have a violent nature to do harm onto our fellow humans as well as to all living things around us. I don't mean to include the act of killing, slaughtering, and eating of animal flesh, but the torture of animals such as what we may call a pet or even a wild animal as well. We have violent crimes such as rape and murder. Our specie preys upon our own week with greedy intentions by cheating, lying, and stealing. It is deep in our nature, it is what makes us the top of the food chain, and we will never, ever change until we become extinct ourselves.

As I pointed out earlier, we as human beings may try to care about the world around us until our comfort zone becomes threatened. Then, we don't care about what it takes to get back to our comfort zone. We don't care what dirty deals go on behind closed doors, or who lives or dies, as long as we get back to our comfort zone. It is human nature and defines us as who we really are. It helped us crawl out of the wilderness and walk upright on our two feet and dominate the world we call home, our Earth.

If you take a close look at our own history, we have to rely on someone's interpretation of what was written, or in the artifacts that were found. It is still a guessing game at best. Everyone has their own views and it should be respected, considering that humans have a relatively short life expectancy and there were no eye witnesses to rely on to tell us about our past. Even if there were absolute proof of a distinct fact, time has a way of distorting the facts.

A good way to look at history is to look at the present times and how things are now, here and in the parts of the world in which the history you would be looking at had occurred in. In different parts of the world some people are treated differently than in other parts. For example; in the Middle East a woman is not allowed to walk beside or in front of a man, rather only allowed to stay two steps back. In the US there is no such rule, although most men don't act like a gentleman and allow a lady to walk in front when entering a room. Most men will usually walk in front of the lady they are with. Maybe it is a "Macho" thing, subconsciously enacted to protect the weaker specie by making sure the room being entered is safe.

In pretty much every place around the world, women are considered in a cultural sense to be beneath all men. Yes, there are some men who place a woman above a man, such as my self, but everyone has heard of the "Glass Ceiling" when it comes to corporate structure. Yes, men in general are physically stronger, but that only means crap. Men at times think with their "Balls", and women don't have the luxury, but can make the same stupid decisions.

When humans first walked upright it was a good bet that males were the dominate gender. It pertained to breeding rights and protection of the group, and we only have to look at our close relatives, the primates, to see this. It allowed the strongest and possibly the smartest to continue our specie, and to help push us forward into evolving into our present state.

As humans developed into a more civilized society, creating villages and communities, and eventually building larger towns and cities, we didn't change all that much. Our leaders were either voted or accepted as such by their ability to bring together and coordinate all those around them to perform whatever task at hand, and in most cases they took control by force, the general masses outside of their following. The strongest and/ or the smartest became the leaders and pushed our specie then, farther into being more civilized. When that leader couldn't keep control of his followers, they were overthrown and eventually through time we advanced into what we are today. No difference in then, our present state, or back when we first walked upright. Human nature hasn't changed and as we took two or three steps forward we took a step back, every time.

As we grew smarter, as we learned to make and use tools to perform tasks or to use to hunt or to defend, we started to acquire possessions. In some family units and in some small communities, we shared pretty much everything. We had to in order to survive. It would be a good bet we even shared our mates. The more we grew in population, the more we mingled with others from different groups, the more we didn't share. As this became a more common practice of not sharing, it would eventually lead to greed and selfishness. In turn, this led to fighting and to wars.

Humans are unique for an animal, as in by being self aware. We pondered the thought of Life and Death and we sought for the truth of the unknown. Most of the time we learned from our mistakes, but our greed even limited that avenue. We became very imaginative, which furthered the evolution into being more creative and more inventive. The problem with this is that with our more advanced sense of imagination and inventiveness, the more we became fearful of the unknown. With knowledge, we opened our eyes to more unknown.

When you look at all of the dynamics that make us Human, it becomes understandable why we became so religious.

Take into consideration that;

1. We pray on the weak, including our own
2. We are filled with greed, to acquire everything we can before someone else does
3. We will manipulate those that we can to acquire what we desire
4. We will utilize the fact of the fear of the unknown to overpower and manipulate those that we can to get what we desire
5. We will "Lie, Cheat, and Steal" whenever we have to in order to survive

It is only Human Nature and is our driving force that put us on the top of the food chain and become the dominating force of all living things. We in ourselves have become our own Gods. We helped in creating life out of unnatural means, through selective, medically manipulated means, and we have taken life and made it become extinct. If a God is truly "Omnipotent" then, we have become that by eliminating all of our own natural Predacious Enemies. The only enemy we have now is ourselves. So, Gods we have truly become.

If you think about any religion and where and when it originated, you have to wonder how it started. First, look at the time frame in which it was conceived. Before Jesus of Nazareth was even born many religions had come and gone. Sumerians had their beliefs as well as the Greeks, Egyptians, and Romans. The world was ruled in parts by large and small Empires that came and went. Civilizations were bullied and forced to bow down to whoever was the prevailing ruler then. The somewhat wealthy kissed the wealthier asses to try to keep what wealth they had, and the poor did all of the work for very little. If you became sick you couldn't work and probably died. Children were bought and sold or traded like livestock. The children of the poor were even forced to work pretty much as soon as they could walk and understand that they had to do something for someone else in order to eat. The only ones who didn't have it so bad were the ones who had some wealth.

If you do not think that it was this bad, then take a trip and stay in a poor country, in one of its villages or in the poorer parts of its cities and stay there for a month or so, living amongst these people. Then, tell me that I'm not correct in that life then wasn't as I've stated it was. When you sit in your comfortable home with your comforting possessions you can thank the continuous evolution of society for making it so. If you had followed my advice and spent a month in a poor village you would have a view into the past. Things haven't changed much over time in some places.

Two thousand years ago or so, it was a tough place to live. Women were basically slaves along with the children. Men ruled their families with a heavy hand. There were very strict laws with severe punishments. For example, you could lose a hand if you were caught stealing, which meant the wrist was burned to stop the bleeding after the hand was chopped off. A child or wife couldn't work as well with one hand rather than with two. So, a father or husband had to be strict with his family. There were thieves of course, but they were the ones that had no other means of earning food.

Amongst the thieves were also con artists. "To con someone" wasn't invented in recent times; it is probably as old as the oldest profession, if not older. If I can trick you into thinking that what I'm offering to trade you with is worth a lot more than it actually is, so you would think it is as equal to or worth more to what I want from you, then I just conned you. It is an easy concept and has been used for a few thousand years.

Now let's say that back then you met someone who spoke to you of a belief that was very similar to most of the religions that existed then, with a few minor differences. The person you were listening to was very charismatic and was able to grab your attention by telling you things you wanted to hear. Such as; if you sinned all of your life you could be forgiven by repenting and accepting this God as the only one. Add to the fact that in those times it was common belief that when you die there was an after life. If you were a sinner and didn't repent you would go to a very terrible place for eternity. If you repented and believed in this God you would go to a very nice place.

Since no one has actually proven that they have been to any of these places and has come back to testify to it, that it is a fact and not fiction, and therefore it is another unknown. It is just another ploy to use to con someone with. When life as you know it sort of sucks and you would like to believe that another place exists that is much better for you, you would give your attention to anyone who will tell you that it does exist. Especially if they tell you with lots of enthusiasm that it does exist as if they had been there personally or knew someone that had.

Stories are very easily started and expanded upon over time. Start a rumor at your place of work or in your inner circle of friends and give it a little time to get back to you and see how much it changes and how many people believe it is the truth. Imagine if it had a thousand years or more to be told and retold. As P.T. Barnum was erroneously quoted as saying; "There's a sucker born every minute", no matter who said it, it is still the plain and simple fact. Humans will believe anything if told in the right manner.

Now as I've stated earlier that written history doesn't necessarily state all of the facts, because those who could write then could have been influenced by force or by wealth. Those who could write were educated and most likely from some form of wealth and therefore you would be reading what they wrote through their eyes and not necessarily from those who were involved in the historic event that couldn't write and were poor. Through their eyes history may have been a little different.

It is very much possible that a mere carpenter saw another man preaching to a crowd that he could wash away their sins by dunking their bodies in the river, that he was the key holder and the river was the lock into a better after life. Whether this carpenter believed this other man or not it was a good way to earn a place to sleep for the night and receive some food as well. It was better than working for a mere living.

Somewhere along the way there grew a following of people who actually believed in the preaching. Even the ones doing the preaching might have started believing in their own scam when they saw how moved and motivated their followers had become. Take a look at modern times with the different cults that have made the news. Jim Jones and David Koresh had followers that believed in them so much that they died for them. Heaven's Gate is another group that was willing to die for their religion.

Sometimes a fantasy world becomes too much of an escape out of reality that it becomes that person's reality. All of us do it to some extent. I fantasize being a sports hero or rock star when I'm by myself exercising and shooting hoops, or singing along in the truck or car to the radio. To most people life could always be better and it was probably exactly like that ever since humans first could process an intelligent and progressive thought.

Religion is something that has been a very big part of Human Development. It has shaped our personality, pointed us in directions, governed our lives, and has been as much of a part as being the Human Nature as greed has been. There has been and continues to be many who believe in their religion to the extreme point that they will even kill to express their point.

Islamic Extremists are no different than those Missionaries that went into the wilderness to convert the Indigenous People, "Savages" that believed in a more primitive way. The Missionaries brought with them common diseases that were mortally fatal to the isolated people of these villages and in some cases they wiped out (killed) a group of people that shouldn't have died. Extinction or Genocide, or an act of God, you can call it what you will but I call it "Arrogance" and I don't see any difference between Religious Jihad that Muslim Extremists follow and Christian Missionaries practice. Ignorance is bliss if you hide behind it, but the problem with all of Society is that there is No Accountability!

Look at the world today and tell me if anything has changed. You have a major religion that is dominant in its own part of the world vying for dominance amongst the others. They all want a piece of the pie and the most stupid thing they all have in common is that they all preach family values, treat everyone else as you would want them to treat you, and that there is only one God. What seems so stupid is that they all are so arrogant that they each feel that their "shit doesn't stink". As an outsider's point of view they all look to be praying to the same God, whether it is some Supreme Being or all living things as a One Collective Life Force. I hate to be too sarcastic, but who cares.

In this country we have as part of our Constitution that we have the freedom to believe in a religion of our choosing. Although Christianity is the accepted religion of this country by the use of the Christian Bible in our court houses, on our currency, and among other things, there is supposed to be a separation of church and state. Yes, the American People are very arrogant and we are no different than any other country. In our history there have been cross burnings in the name of God, hangings, and even church burnings. Somewhere in all bibles is the preaching of respect on to others. Apparently that sermon was missed on that day by those who practice hate, prejudice, and violence. Again, I emphasize the fact that it is Human Nature to see only the things one wants to see.

In my life I have seen a few Religious Cults come in the area and go. Bible Speaks, Sun Myung Moon, and a couple more, have come and gone in my area at some point. A close friend of mine was a witness in hiding, to what a few men in white sheets and hoods can do to a tree and a rope, and a live human. I've listened to the voices of prejudice and hate volley out their beliefs, and not just about one side, but of that from the other side as well. I've visited a couple of Catholic Monasteries and witnessed how well the Bishops, the Priests, and there understudies lived and ate while their followers lived in poverty and their leader lives like a king as well. I watch as month after month Muslim Extremists are willing and actually go ahead with blowing themselves up in trying to, and kill other human beings, some of which are Muslims as well.

I've watched on the television news broadcasts as genocide was carried out in some of the countries around the world, and I ask myself for what? Is it in the name of God that these atrocities are carried out? Whose God are they following? If this so called "Omnipotent" God that each and every religion believes in is so powerful that it influences these atrocities, then why do innocent children die of cancer and of starvation? Why are and have throughout our past as a civilization have women been raped, sometimes their breasts cut from their bodies, and sometimes they are murdered? Is this so called God a representation of our own Human Psyche?

For those who find what I've have written a little offensive, then I really don't apologize for anything. All of the excuses you put forward do not explain the reality of it all. They are only excuses to explain the unknown, the un-provable. An all caring, all forgiving, all powerful God would not allow any of this to exist if this so called "God" did truly exist. If you can't search your inner self and find the truth then you are deeply caught up in their scare tactics of your religion and are merely one sheep in a flock of many that needs a Sheppard to tell you when to eat and when to sleep, when to walk and when to run, when to shit and when to be afraid. If you believe that by committing a "Religious Jihad", or carrying out a suicide bombing, that in your after life you will be blessed with many virgins for your pleasure, then you have been conned. You might as well play with yourself, because that is the only action from a virgin you'll get, just before and long after you die!

Again, I have to remind you that the way things are now in some countries is probably the way they were for a few thousand years. For those future suicide bombers, what if you really were conned and you just wasted your life for nothing and possible killed very innocent people, or even perhaps someone who could have changed the world for the better? Maybe even the next Messiah might be one of your next unfortunate victims.

Would an All Caring and All Powerful God allow a Catholic Priest to molest and have sex with a child or a teenager? If the Catholic Church wasn't so quick to cover it up and hide away its own Priests that did such an unforgivable sin, then one would think that the Catholic Church was a viable avenue to its God. Now I have to ask, is this God, the same God that is this Great Supreme Being that they boast about, then why the cover up? I have to look at the common sense point of view and believe that there is no after life and therefore no hell. If there was, then the Catholic Church's Leaders wouldn't cover any of this up because it is a sin to lie, and the church leaders seem to not fear hell.

My friend the plumber will state that he isn't religious to the extreme that most people are and that he doesn't believe in any form of an after life. He believes that Heaven and Hell are here and now and can testify that he has been there in both places. He has seen birth and has seen death. He has lived in hell when his wife's Visa was denied and through his depressive and oppressed state he thought he would have to give up his way of life here and hide out in the mountainous jungles of his wife's country. He told me that Hell is a place he wouldn't even wish on his enemies. My friend the plumber has clearly stated that he does not believe in an after life, but just in case, Satan better beware and fear him, for my friend the plumber goes down for no one.

It would be great if there were no wars, no poverty, no pressure for accumulation of wealth and without any wealth to accumulate, no incurable diseases, no hate, no prejudices, no crimes. It would be wonderful if there were a place where everyone lived as an equal and allowed to believe in the faith of their own choice. Everyone worked to the betterment of our planet and to our civilization. All were held completely accountable and no one told any lies. We didn't cheat and steal and we respected everyone else's life and opinions. But then again, I've slipped into my fantasy world again. I believe that John Lennon wrote a song about this as well.

I believe that there is something there that can only be explained as a form of God. When you feel Love in your heart, when you hold your child or children close, the joy that is felt can only be explained as something special. When indeed a child is brought into this world it has to be some form of a hand of God to create such a miracle. Even the creation of life on this planet is a miracle that it happened.

All Humans need some form of hope to believe in, it is a part of our nature. Without our planet we call Earth we would not exist. It gave us life and feeds us and shelters us. Maybe the Indigenous People around the world had it right, that our Earth is our Mother. Maybe God really stands for Mother Earth. Maybe we should take better care of her and all that reside with her as she has taken care of us.

Maybe we all should step back and look deeply into our own souls and decide if it is truly a God we believe in and follow its word, or are we following the ambitions of a few men with greed on their minds and scams at their hands. If our Gods are so great, then why don't they talk to us individually in person and not depend on some religious figure to act as a go between? We shouldn't be praying to the "God Almighty Dollar", which it seems that it has come down to. My friend the plumber says that the answers are all around each and every one of us. We know what is right in our own hearts and we know that we need to respect others as we would want them to respect our own selves.

The Marriage Issue

As I've stated before, I have been around for a long time. I am married and I personally don't see what the big deal about marriage is all about. I would like to know who gave only the religious groups the sole rights to marriage. The last I knew a couple could go to a church of their faith and talk with that church's religious leader and arrange to have the marriage ceremony in that place of worship and performed by an ordained person of that religion. OR, the happy couple could go to the Justice of the Peace and have an informal ceremony. OR, have a ship's Captain perform the ceremony on his ship.

Anyway, the happy couple still had to go through the local government and get a Marriage License to make it all legal. So, therefore, the Government is the one who have the biggest say in the make up of a marriage. Now, the Government has made it a law that it is Illegal to Discriminate. Again, I ask, "What is the Issue Here?"

Let us look deep into the issue that has everyone so divided. Long ago in the past and it still happens in the present, a family would make an arrangement with another family to join in marriage a boy/man and a girl/woman. The reason for this was probably that the children were the property of their parents. The parents' beliefs were that they spent all of this time and all of the expenses to raise this child since conception and they should get their just pay for it as well, whether it would be in livestock, land, food, currency, and/or prestige, whatever. We eventually evolved out of Mid Evil Times and allowed our children to "choose" a spouse. Usually it was a mutual agreement between the happy couple, with the exception of the common "Shotgun Wedding", but here in the U.S. a Male and a Female Human were allowed to choose their spouse.

As one would look around the world and even in this country as well, there are still societies that are still in the Dark Ages. They still make arrangements for their children's spouses. Why, there are even Religions that choose a certain man to marry a certain woman who are in their congregation or from another in that faith and are both single. The woman doesn't have the right to choose, but her fellow worshipers do the choosing for her. There are even societies that choose a spouse for another so the children will hopefully have the "Proper Genes" to continue creating a "Better Race of Humans".

We are now in Modern Times and a lot has been learned about the Human Mind and Physiology. We are supposed to have evolved into a society that believes in "Having a Choice", "Speaking Our Mind", "Religious Freedom", Freedom From Persecution", "Freedom of Sexual Orientation", We are supposed to have Evolved into a Society of Intelligence, of Compassion, of Understanding, and of Reasoning. Then why are we not? Why then is there so much Greed, and Hatred, and Prejudice when it comes to who is allowed to marry who?

One of the base Building Blocks that this Country's foundation was built upon was to offer a Sanctuary from Persecution. I will admit that although this Nation at times has failed to live up to this very high expectation, we have evolved to better ourselves to not make those mistakes again. It sickens me to see Religious Groups, as well as Arrogant Others claim that a Marriage can only be between a Man and a Woman. "<u>Who the Hell are You</u>" to cram Your Beliefs down everybody else's throat. You are not God and this is not Mid Evil Times. People like you are the fuel that will start what you fear the most, and that is your Armageddon. This country was based on Freedoms. One being of Freedom of Religion, meaning, you believe in what you want to and I believe in what I want to, and the Government will remain NEUTRAL! Don't preach to me if I don't ask you to and I won't preach to you if you don't ask me to.

In most Bibles there are statements referring to respecting others, and it is a sin to disrespect them in any way. Forcing your beliefs upon someone else is disrespecting them. If two wrongs don't make a right, then in your beliefs that same sex love is a sin, therefore that sin and your sin of interfering doesn't make it right either.

If a person finds another person attractive and both persons love each other and are devoted to each other, and are willing to pledge their love for one another, then they should have the right to get married, whether in a church that is willing to marry them or by the Justice of the Peace if that is what they wish to do. Love is love. It is something that is felt deep inside your heart. It has no boundaries, no limits. Love sees no color or sexual characteristics. It's a deep caring about another's feelings. It's a devotion to be with that person till the end of time. I've been married to my wife for over twenty years and am raising our children to be intelligent, to be understanding, and compassionate. Not to be blind and selfish.

In our Society we do have some rules and laws to abide by, which are basically there to protect others from harm, but we have also rules and laws that are supposed to protect our rights of freedom. In public there are compromises to certain displays of our beliefs and way of life. That is called respect and consideration. If the way we choose to live our life does not cross these boundaries in public, if what we choose to do with our lives is not forced upon someone else, then there should be no complaints. How we live our lives in private, and again, as long as our beliefs are not forced upon anyone else, then its no one else's business.

Everyone out there has their life to live. It is theirs and no one else. No one can live your life for you. You have to live it yourself. You have to look yourself in the eye every day and be happy with your life, because it is who you are. You can not worry what anyone else thinks about you. You are the only one that can be happy with your life. If you are not, then change your life.

If a man and a woman love each other and want to get married, then they have the right to. If a man and another man love each other and want to get married, then they have the right to. If a woman and another woman love each other and want to get married, then they have the right to. For those that oppose my thoughts, then all I can say is it's not your life to live. Stop trying to live other people's lives. You really don't want me coming into your home and running your life, do you?

The Illegal Immigration Issue

The Immigration issue is not as simple as it may seem to some. On one hand, our borders are a sham and if you look at border laws in some of the other countries around the world, a violator could be shot for trespassing by being accused of Spying. On the other hand, when do you say enough is enough? When the "Land of Plenty" has started to run dry and its inhabitants are feeling the pinch of global financial despair?

In Colonial Times, the Americas were a place of refuge for some and a place to seek fortune in a land of plenty for others. Though the lands of the Americas were taken by acquisition through force from the native population, and later the native populations were treated as non-citizens, masses of immigrants still flocked to these shores for the same two reasons. A plaque resides with the Statue of Liberty that states;

> "Not like the brazen giant of Greek fame,
> With conquering limbs astride from land to land;
> Here at our sea-washed, sunset gates shall stand
> A mighty woman with a torch, whose flame
> Is the imprisoned lightning, and her name
> Mother of Exiles. From her beacon-hand
> Glows world-wide welcome; her mild eyes command
> The air-bridged harbor that twin cities frame.
> "Keep, ancient lands, your storied pomp!" cries she
> 'With silent lips. "Give me your tired, your poor,
> Your huddled masses yearning to breathe free,

The wretched refuse of your teeming shore.
Send these, the homeless, tempest-tossed to me,
I lift my lamp beside the golden door!"

With this we have welcomed millions to this country to start a new life. Yes, in many cases, immigrants that have come here have found a better way of life than from where they had come from. The appeal of being apart of a nation that proudly boasts "We are the Land of the Free, and the Home of the Brave" does have a certain appeal. We are a place where civil rights is much better than most places around the world. We are a place where a poor person can come into this country and earn much more money than in the country they have left, and to some it is a way to financially support your family you have left behind.

True Americans for the most part are arrogant, selfish, compassionate, sometimes understanding, and critical to all of those who are not American. We Americans of the United States even view Canadians as inferior, which proves are arrogance. After all, both Canada and the United States are both in North America, and we here in the U.S. call ourselves Americans. I can state this as a fact because I look and listen to what all of those around me have to say, and through my many trips into other countries. I have seen typical Americans as they are in other countries act like they own the place and disrespect the people of that country.

To me, witnessing this makes me feel ashamed that I am an American, but that is what defines us as an American, we are what we are. We hear something bad about someone, and right away we are quick to condemn all of those who are even only remotely related to that individual. As an example; a few Americans are treated rudely in France, so therefore, all of the French are considered rude. A small group of Native Americans protest against the State Department for not living up to the treaties that were agreed upon, and all Native Americans are considered trouble makers. A group of Muslim Radicals attack us on our own soil, and all Muslims are considered Radicals.

I suppose that if we as a nation didn't let our "Big Business Companies" go into other countries and plunder their resources and the people of those countries weren't crapped on as such, we probably wouldn't be viewed upon nor treated as we are. Then again, we wouldn't be one of the, if not the wealthiest nations in the world. We wouldn't be "Arrogant

Americans". We wouldn't be having an immigration problem. We might not be considered the "Land of Plenty".

Part of our problem with our "Loose Borders" is the trafficking of illegal narcotics across our borders. If you compared how many people died from the 911 attack to all of those that have died from the use, the trafficking, and the collateral damage of innocent people in and around the drug trade, the 911 attack would seem like a drop in a bucket. We have been under attack for decades by the illegal drug trade.

Our own Government was involved in the trafficking of illegal drugs with the Contra Scandal and could very well be still involved. We turn a blind eye to some of the heroin traffickers in Afghanistan and Pakistan who help the Governments of those countries in the war on terrorism. Our Government keeps many secrets from its own people. We declared war in a blink of an eye on the Muslim Community over the 911 Attack. And please don't get me wrong, we had to hold the right people accountable and do something. I disapprove how it was "Half Assed" handled, which is why we are currently in the Middle East engaged in a war. So tell me why we haven't declared all out war on illegal drug trafficking considering many, many more people have died in the wake of it all? Who is benefitting from the trafficking of illegal drugs?

This nation has specific laws about immigration. "We the People" didn't write the laws, our government officials did. Our government enforces most of all of the other laws they came up with. Don't pay your taxes and find out how quick they come to collect with interest or throw you in jail and take all of your possessions away from you. Yet there are those that are here illegally and don't pay their taxes and are not pursued. I just don't understand the double standard. Who is profiting over this? Be late with a couple of loan or credit card payments and your credit is black listed. As an adult, don't wear your seat belt and get caught and you get ticketed and fined. My point is if there is a law prohibiting an act and a punishment for that breaking of that law, then it should be enforced.

Again, don't get me wrong, I do feel empathy for those who have come into this country illegally to work hard to earn money to help support their families. A person has to do what they have to, so as they and their family can survive. During these financially troubling times most of us have had to adjust to lower incomes and living with the thought that it could get worse and we could end up losing what little we have left. Every human being on this planet should be allowed to live free from persecution, have a respectable job and live a comfortable life style, and all human beings should be treated the same fair way as all other human beings with no one being treated better or worse, but that would be an ideal world and probably an unreal dream.

One solution would be to tell the Mexican Government to hand over its land to become a part of the United States. This would place all Mexican People as citizens of the United States. This would eliminate a considerable amount of land border that would need to be patrolled. It would lessen considerably the influx of illegal immigration. It would allow our law enforcement agencies to eliminate most of the corruption. It would allow our "Big Businesses" to plunder Mexico's resources, if they aren't already doing so. It would allow more coastal waters to be turned into resort and vacation areas. It seems that the possibilities are almost endless. Then again, our government can't seem to do a good enough job running what nation we have without problems, let alone adding half again more to the mix.

Another solution is to completely enforce the laws we have on the books, and also declare war on the trafficking of illegal drugs into this country. My personal feeling is to go a few steps further and accept the fact that there are families that are already here where as one or both parents are here illegally and have children that have been born here as well.

The laws should be changed so as to no longer accept the birth right of a child that is born on this soil if the mother is here illegally. All those that were born here before this law is passed will fall under a different law as long as the Mother;

1. has no criminal back ground
2. declares that she is here illegally
3. medically proves she is the parent of the child or children in question
4. registers and remains as a permanent resident alien and can never become a citizen of the United States
5. becomes employed as a legal, tax paying employee of a legitimate company or self employed, whether part time or full time, and remains employed as such until financially secure enough to retire

The father of the child can fall under the same criteria if he;
1. has no criminal back ground
2. declares that he is also here illegally
3. medically proven he is the father
4. lives with the mother of the child or children in question as a respectable family until his timely death
5. registers and remains as a permanent resident alien and can never become a citizen of the United States
6. becomes employed as a legal, tax paying employee of a legitimate company or self employed, whether part time or full time, and remains employed as such until financially secure enough to retire

If either parent does not follow these simple rules, then they are deported back to their country of origin.

Those that are here illegally that are not the parent of any child born in the United States before the new laws are passed as well as after, will be rounded up, and imprisoned for a year for the first violation, two years for the second, and ten years to life for the third. Also, for each person caught and imprisoned and for each year of their imprisonment of each illegal alien, the government of citizenship of that individual will pay a fine to cover the costs of the arresting, conviction, and imprisonment for that individual. If the country of citizenship for an individual refuses to pay, then all trade dealings with that country will be immediately stopped, no exclusions. There should also be a substantial penalty of fines and prison time for those individuals as well as those companies that hire illegal immigrants.

All of this may seem harsh to you, but think about why people are illegally coming to this country. Most illegal immigrants live under the radar by either doing work that most Americans don't want to do for very low wages and by taking work from our professional tradesmen by doing it a lot cheaper and in most cases doing very much sub standard work. They do the work cheaper and earn low wages because they are not paying taxes and they live in sub standard conditions. We became a wealthy nation by being aggressive, by being hard working, determined, by being financially smart, and yes, a little greedy.

Standards were placed into effect for a reason to protect the public from hazards. My friend the plumber has told me that in Massachusetts, the Plumbing Codes contain certain rules and methods that are in place to protect the safety of the people in that home, building, and that community. If violated, these wrong practices could endanger a family or a community. Such as, if there were no back flow prevention devise on a hydronic boiler and if the water main in the street or the water supply pipe coming out of an individual's well were to break, then contaminated un-potable water could be siphoned out of the boiler and contaminate the water supply, causing people to become sick and possible death. Our professional tradesmen learned the state and national codes pertaining to their professions, they did their apprenticeships, and they follow the rules to remain a responsible and qualified tradesman. They have earned their way to work in their profession, not the unqualified illegal immigrant.

My friend on various occasions has encountered many situations where a homeowner had hired someone who was unlicensed, didn't speak English all that well, and did the work very cheap, and the work that they did could endanger the life of the family living there and possibly the neighborhood.

If countries around the world can't keep their citizens employed and healthy, then they should ask for and allow some form of help to allow them to prosper. If they have the ways and means to and they refuse to help their population, then the world should step in and force them to. I am not against people immigrating to the United States or even elsewhere, I am against it being done illegally. What's fare is fare. If you don't like the country you are from and a citizen of, do everything in your power to change that country to make it a better place for <u>all</u> of its citizens. That is what I am trying to do here.

If places like Mexico and China had a government and a military that wasn't so corrupt, and they cared enough about their people that they did create plenty of honest, decent paying jobs, the United States wouldn't have the illegal immigration problem we are having.

If these countries forced the companies inside of its borders to produce high quality products, paid their workers decent wages and good benefits, and didn't force them to work long hours in an unsafe work environment, then a Mexican or a Chinese worker can be proud of the work and product they are producing. Then their people would be happy to remain in their country of origin. Now don't get me wrong. As I have stated, I am not against Immigration to this country by anyone. I am against it done illegally.

In early American times, our Government had plans to expand its borders, thus, the big push to the west coast. As the plaque states on Ellis Island, the Government wanted masses of people to help infiltrate and settle the lands west of the Mississippi, much in the same manner as the Jewish people did to create Israel. Now, we don't have the land to further settle. If we keep turning our woodlands into towns and cities, into farms and factories, the land that was America will no longer be as free as we believe that we are. So again, I ask you, when is enough, enough?

The world is being over populated as is. We are no longer in Mid-Evil Times where a child had a twenty percent chance of making it to adulthood, not to mention to die a ripe old age of Fifty. China has tried to enforce a one child per family rule. Most South American Countries are strong Catholic believers and the catholic Religion preaches families need many children. This is absurd and should no longer be practiced. This planet is running out of room. Our Oceans are already showing declines in marine life. Our air is already heavy with "Greenhouse Gases". Ironically, all of the major religions of the world basically preach "Armageddon" if we keep on sinning, and it is our overpopulating our planet that is becoming our downfall, which may very well be the Armageddon they are preaching. Overpopulation brings on more poverty and more desire to have what someone else has, which leads to violent crimes.

If we put an end to illegal immigration by strictly enforcing a good Immigration Policy, then we will force Mexico to have to deal with their problem of too many people and not enough work for all of them!

The Role of the United Nations

WHEN THE UNITED Nations Organization was first formed to replace the League of Nations, which didn't live up to expectations, was supposed to be a world organization that would co-ordinate cooperation between countries involving international law, international security, economic development, social progress, human rights, and above all else, world peace. This sounds pretty good if only it actually did happen, but if you look around the world you see that it basically boils down to, if the World Powers can't gain anything out of it, they don't want to get involved and the world remains as corrupt and violent as usual. A few good examples are the problems with North Korea and Iran developing nuclear weapons and allowing India and Pakistan to develop nuclear weapons as well. After the devastating effects of the Hiroshima and the Nagasaki atomic bombings to bring to an end of World War Two, the United Nations' first priority should have been to band all nuclear weapons from ever being made.

I understand the theory behind the threat of having and the threat of defensively using these world destroying weapons, which is basically saying that if you attack me I will destroy you, or threatening with a terrible war to keep the peace. Another good example would be someone carrying and displaying a big gun to ward off a "would be mugger" or thief. Carrying a big gun and accumulating weapons of mass destruction are two very big differences. Personally, I think its one of the most stupid ideas Mankind has ever come up with, which shows our greed so much that we are willing to destroy the world just to keep anyone from taking it over. If our United Nations had half of the integrity and accountability it was created to have, then there would never be another nuclear weapon made after the two dropped in Japan in 1945.

If the United Nations performed its intended duties there wouldn't be genocide taking place in a few countries in Africa and as well in Myanmar. Human rights violations would not take place in China. Human trafficking would be non-existing. The plundering of a country's natural resources would never happen. Starvation and disease would not exist, or would there ever be a war in the Middle East that would be never ending. The role the United Nations was to intervene on worldly problems and act as a mediator to resolve any differences, but they have failed miserably and have become a Nation in itself revolving around the greed and wealth of Big Businesses that seem to be running the world. I think it is about time the United Nations starts living up to the World's People's expectations. "Shit or get off of the pot!"

Gun Control

I OWN A few guns and I am a hunter of wild animals. Not only because of my Native American heritage, but because of my desire for the frill of the hunt and the enjoyment of eating animal flesh are the reasons I hunt. I also am fascinated in the power, simplicity, and the beauty of a well made firearm as a weapon and as a work of art. There is something about a gun stock made of a piece of wood, that was so finely crafted with a "fiddle back" texture of wood grain that is beautiful to look at.

I was raised by my father around guns and hunting. I was taught since the age of four to always, at all times, know where the muzzle of my gun is always pointing. It should never be pointed at another human being and to always be mindful to all areas around you. There might be someone unseen in those areas, or even a house. It didn't take too many swift boots to my ass to learn this rule. Through time I have raised my children the same way.

Since they were old enough to walk with me they carried their pop guns, as I did at that age, as we walked through the woods around our home. I showed them how to track wild game, how to determine your location by the sounds around you, the lay of the land, and by the sky, how to feel all of nature around you and to be one with your surroundings. They learned to understand that the direction of the muzzle of their pop gun was pointing in was very important to the safety of those around them. That once you pull that trigger, you can never pull that bullet back. These are words of wisdom that my father ingrained into my soul, and I have ingrained into my children's as well.

As I watch the television shows and the news, and I see all of the violence that exists in the world today, and a lot of this in our own country,

I am caught in the middle of the NRA advocates and the gun restriction activists. I believe that everyone has the right to defend themselves against violence, whether their home is being violently broken into or there is physical, brutal harm being imposed upon their person or their close loved ones. I have been in a few of these situations before. How I have reacted is that of my own personal business and no one else's. I did what I felt was necessary to negate the situation.

As my father has stated that once you pull that trigger, you can never pull back that bullet, and that you should always treat every gun as if it were loaded. Never point a gun unless you are prepared to pull that trigger and kill that upon which you are pointing at! Before you have pulled that trigger, you should have already decided to accept the consequences for your actions! These are my words of wisdom and I strongly suggest these thoughts to all of those that decide to point a gun and pull the trigger, no matter if it is loaded or not.

As of now there are decent laws in place in most states that do make a potential gun buyer jump through hoops, but they do basically weed out those who have a questionable criminal background. I do have to agree that some of the laws pertaining to guns in the home are a bit overboard, but I grew up differently than most children and so have my children.

My father never locked up his guns. Being a part time farmer it was necessary to be able to have access to a gun to protect his animals from harm from predatory animals that meant to kill or do harm to his animals. I have always felt the same. Personally, I would feel very stupid if someone had broken into my home while I was asleep and I had to fumble around in the dark trying to unlock a gun safe to use my gun to protect my family. My children were taught, as was I, to never play with a real gun. If they or I ever wanted to touch or look at a real gun, all that was needed was to ask permission and my father or my self would supervise it to make sure that the basic rules of gun safety were followed.

1. Treat every gun as a real gun, even if it is a toy gun
2. Treat every gun as if it were loaded, even if you have already checked it and it is not loaded
3. Never point a gun at anything, unless you are prepared to pull the trigger and accept the consequences
4. Understand the fact that once you pull the trigger, you can never pull back the bullet

I have known some associates that have been able to acquire weapons of all sorts easily through gun shows held in certain states that have limited gun laws. I have been told that it is virtually very easy for anyone to purchase just about any form of gun there and that conversion methods and how to obtain conversion kits to change a semi automatic into a fully automatic are also readily available there as well. Now this is where I have to disagree with the NRA. There is a point to where you are hunting wild game and hunting for humans. A gun for the purpose of stalking and killing a wild animal for sport and/or for food is one very type of weapon. An assault weapon, something that the Police or Military uses, is totally different and the use of this kind of firearm is for the sole intent purpose of killing or wounding a human being, "no if, and, or buts" about it.

I can kill an animal the size of a human being with a well placed shot from a pellet gun that produces a muzzle velocity of over two hundred and fifty feet per second. A twenty-two caliber pistol is the choice of most professionals because of the ease to make a silencer for and the lethal outcome it produces. A twelve gauge shotgun designed for the sole purpose to hunt deer, pheasant, ducks, geese, and partridge can very easily kill a human being burglar, rapist, murderer that is threatening you or your family, even if it only has birdshot in it. Why even a four-ten shotgun with a round of birdshot can be just as much of a lethal weapon when it comes to killing a perpetrator, if necessary.

So tell me why all of you that "insist on having" assault weapons, or military weapons to defend yourself and your community against the onslaught of Home Invaders, Store Robbers, Criminals, Child Molesters, Rapists, Terrorists, or our own "Socialistic" Government need such "heavy artillery" when a sharp stick, a knife, a pellet gun, or a hunting firearm will suffice? I was trained to utilize anything in my reach as a weapon. I can easily kill a human being with a pencil, a glass bottle, a magazine or phone book, a phone or drapery cord or even a corner of a table or chair if I felt that the situation was life threatening.

The problem is that the bigger the gun the more powerful a person feels. The same scenario applies to those Law Officers when a badge that they wear goes to their head. Power is a very corrupt instrument when a person feels they are above its control, when they feel they have absolute control. I don't feel sorry for those that let power go to their head. All that I can say to them is that when you pull that trigger, you better be ready to accept the consequence for your action because you can never pull that bullet back!

The Local Issues

I AM A simple man that looks at the world around me and sees the things that are good with it. I also see the things that are wrong with it as well. When I see something that is wrong I think of the reasons why it's that way and what it would take to make it better.

For example; I live in New England and we have winter here and with it we have snow covered roads. The snowplows come along, plow and salt the roads, and it dries and grinds down the surface, and even breaks up the road itself. I look at a frost heaved road and know that after ten years or so the town or state will pay for a "Half Assed", or somewhat "Half Assed" repair or resurfacing job. Some of the time the repairing or repaving company takes care of the real problem.

Now I know that the town, city, or state feels that it is much cheaper in the long run to just do the repairs or repaving, but I believe that if you fix the real problem then the repairs won't be necessary for a much longer time to come.

Case in point, my friend the plumber lives on a rural gravel road. For years the town would use a landscape rake to rake up the road and use the loose gravel to fill in the pot holes. They would also only do this the day before or the day of a day or two of rain in the forecast. There is a drainage ditch about three feet wide and between one and two feet deep along the East side of the road where his driveway is. The road for a good half mile is some what level in grade with a slight downhill pitch towards the South. Every time the Town Road Crew would rake it they would leave a hump, or wind row between the drainage ditch and the side of the road so the rain water would not have a way to get into the drainage ditch.

My friend would drive his tractor up the road from his driveway and with the loader attached to the front he would dig out a break into the wind row so the water would be allowed to flow into the drainage ditch. He would make about two or three of these breaks and it would stop the rain water from running down the side of the road and washing out the end of his driveway to get into the drainage ditch.

Now you would think that the Town Road Crew would be raking the road before a substantial rain and using the excuse that it will keep the dust down and help pack the loose gravel quicker. In fact, it made the pot holes return for two reasons. One; they didn't use the road grader to scrape the gravel down below the bottom of the pot holes, and Two; the gravel soaked up the rain and turned into mud and the cars and trucks drove through it, their tires bouncing over the small rocks in the mud, bouncing and spraying out muddy water and thus, creating the same or even newer pot holes. If they rake the road after the rainy days when a dry stretch was at hand, the gravel will have time to pack into a much smoother surface with every car and truck that traveled this rural road.

Somewhere along the way the Town Road Crew finally figured it out and they even had learned how to scrape away the pot holes with the road grader, scrape away the wind row, and dig out the drainage ditch. One exception is that they didn't do the same thing to the other side of the road and they keep leaving a wind row on that side. When it rains substantially, there is a little stream running down that side of the road because they made a dike that doesn't allow the water to simply flow off of the road.

Now, to drain out the water in the drainage ditch there are culverts of plastic tubes or galvanized steel that cross underground under the road. Every winter the water in the gravel of the road directly over the culvert tubes freezes and expands, rising quicker than the gravel in the road on either side of the culvert tubes. The reason for this is that the gravel in the road over the top of the culvert tubes is usually only a few inches to a couple of feet thick to the top of the tube. The gravel on either side of the culvert tubes is thick with no air space below and it receives some warmth from that thickness. When the temperature drops below freezing the colder air flows through the culvert tubes and assists in freezing the gravel above it. The gravel on either side resists freezing because of the heat radiating effect coming from the depth of the ground at that point. Therefore, the gravel immediately above the culvert tube freezes, expands, and rises, creating a small hump in the road. The gravel on either side resists and doesn't expand and rise at the same rate.

Now the snow plow eventually comes along and eventually scrapes away the higher gravel on the top of the Culvert tube. Traffic on that stretch of road has to deal with a bump in the road until the time comes when it is eventually scraped away.

Then in the spring when the frost leaves the gravel road, the top of the culvert tub is a depression because of the gravel that was scraped away, and the traffic has to contend with a sharp dip in the road until the Road Crew finally comes along and fills it in.

Now if the winter ended up with a deep freeze and got down below the bottom of the culvert tube, then it would eventually raise the tube up into the road. This can even happen to a culvert tube under a paved road. The trick is to install the culvert tubes so the top of the tubes are a foot below the frost line and it should solve the problem.

The City of Pittsfield, which is not far from my home, has some of the worst roads and streets compared to most of the towns in my area. They do the standard half assed patch job every year, or they pay huge sums of money for the two biggest local excavation companies to re-do the road, and in five years or less the roads are buckling and pot holed as before the road work. These companies usually have the sewer manholes re-done and this year there are chunks of black top missing around some of these manholes. It seems to me that someone should build a manhole that is similar to an electrical conduit expansion fitting, the top part anchored in the blacktop road so as to move up and down with the frost movement of the road. It is a wonder that the city isn't sued big time for damages done to vehicles hitting these huge holes.

My friend the plumber has brought up a fact about accountability in his line of work and the lack there of in the companies performing road work. It seems to me he is right in that in his line of work he has to guarantee his work for a year. Have you ever heard of a road construction company going back and repairing their own screw up free of charge? It sounds to me that they do a crappy job to go back and do the repairs for more money. I guess it is job security. I have heard that in Germany, road construction companies have to guarantee their work for twenty years. I don't know if this is true or not, but if a road is built right, with the dynamics of summer heat and winter frost built into the equation, then there shouldn't be a problem with a twenty year guarantee.

Yes, this has been quite the winter, but if you eliminate the moisture from with-in and under a road, the frost won't develop. The problem with Pittsfield is that they may not patch the potholes for a month or more. Some of these potholes are as deep as a third of the height of a normal tire.

Frost heaves in paved roads is basically the same problem. The only cure is to start out below the frost line with a very porous one foot layer of crushed stone, a heavy weight porous fabric covering the stone to allow drainage into the layer of rock, then on top of that your packed gravel before the layers of pavement.

Along both sides and a couple of feet deeper a drainage layer of drainage pipes, crushed stones, porous fabric, and gravel, and at the top tapering sharply away from the side of the road a layer of top soil with a clay mixture. The drainage pipes would channel the water out and away from the roads to one side or the other, or both, depending on the lay of the land. Keep in mind though that most gravel has a considerable amount of clay and silt in it. These two particles make gravel less drainable by helping to trap the water amongst the coarser grains of sand.

Now by using this system of very porous gravel, crushed stone, porous fabric, and drainage pipes the least amount of water could be trapped and thus keeping the roads from the severe harm of frost heaves. Again, this would be considered too expensive to do and so therefore, we end up with half assed patch work every year. I guess that could be considered "Job Security".

Another local issue with the roads is the junction of the road and the bridge expanses. The road expanse of a bridge, where the road goes from one side of the opening to the other, has an arch to it. This is to help the expanses to handle a heavier load with traffic volume. Now the road coming up to the bridge expanses should be level or actually coming upward to the expanses. I can point out several bridges in Dalton, Pittsfield, and a couple of other towns where it is the opposite. The road actually goes down hill to the bridge expanses and creates a sharp bounce of your vehicle if going over twenty miles an hour. To me it does not appear to be rocket science, but then again, what do I know.

You are driving through a traffic lighted intersection and making a left hand turn onto that street. Another vehicle is stopped at a traffic light with their front tires right behind the stop line. They are centered in their lane of traffic, but if you are driving a vehicle towing a trailer, or a vehicle with a long wheel base, you might clip this other vehicle. It seems to me that all stop lines for intersections with traffic lights should be back twenty feet or more from the intersection. I have even noticed that even on truck route roads a lot of intersections are not really truck friendly with raised islands, ground based signs, and stop lines too close to the intersection for tractor trailers to proceed through the intersection easily. Some of these intersections were recently re-constructed.

Another thing I have a hard time understanding is why you would have at an intersection with traffic lights, divided lanes for vehicles coming from the same direction and having the left turn lane separate, and the straight through traffic and the right turn traffic in the one and only right lane. If the straight through traffic has to stop anyway along with the left turning traffic, letting them both wait for the traffic light to turn green in the same lane seems to make more sense. The right lane should be for the right turning traffic only and let them utilize the "Right on Red" law. This just might ease up the traffic congestion a little during peak times. Again it is only common sense and not rocket science.

Have you ever been traveling in your vehicle on a road that was two lanes, one going in one direction and the other going in the opposite, and couldn't pass the slower moving vehicle in front of you? We have a few like that in Berkshire County, Route 7 and Route 8. There are wide breakdown lanes on either side of the road, the speed limit is usually fifty or fifty-five, and it seems that whenever you approach a straight away, and there are several long ones, there are several cars coming in the other direction and eliminating any passing attempt. It seems to me that if one of the breakdown lanes were turned into an extra right hand lane on every other straight away, then there would be a separate passing lane for one direction of traffic and on the next straight away the other traffic direction would have their passing lane.

On some roads there are passing lanes for up hill traffic. Why not do the same on flatter roads where there is a lot of traffic flow? It seems to make sense, especially when you are stuck behind a vehicle traveling ten to fifteen miles an hour slower than the speed limit and there are five or more vehicles behind them that can't pass.

I also have no respect for those who drive five to ten miles under the speed limit, until a straight away with passing lines or a passing zone appears. Then the slower moving vehicle speeds up to and sometimes over the speed limit and you run out of room to pass them. Then, when the passing opportunity disappears, they slow back down again. You probably wonder why "Road Rage" exists. Again, it's not rocket science, but what do I know! It may seem funny that some people like to drive in the fast lane, but do so while ten miles under the speed limit. I wish they would get their excitement elsewhere.

Because I live in Berkshire County of Western Massachusetts I strongly believe that we need a North/South four lane, two lanes in each direction, bypass highway from the Connecticut to Vermont border. Too many times I have been stuck behind people in vehicles going ten to twenty miles under the speed limit and there are no places to pass this slow moving vehicle. Too many times I needed to get through Gt. Barrington, Stockbridge, Pittsfield, Adams, and N. Adams to get somewhere else and was stuck in bumper to bumper slow moving traffic, and couldn't do anything about it. I am definitely sure I am not the only one who has been through it and agrees with me.

When Lenox allowed a bypass everyone thought that the businesses of Lenox were going to have to close because no one would be passing through the town and stopping to shop. Well, Lenox is doing pretty good despite the bypass and I am sure if one was built now to allow traffic to not get caught in traffic jambs in the towns and cities of Berkshire County, then none of their businesses will dry up and disappear either.

On another subject of local problems, in my state of Massachusetts involving our educational programs, the state tried to hold its teachers a little more accountable. They came up with a testing format to see where each student of Massachusetts is academically at, before he or she graduates high school. This sounded like a good idea and if a student or school were not up to the level of learning they should be at, then the school and/ or teacher(s) should be held somewhat accountable. After all, no matter where you work, if you can't do your job correctly, then you will probably be replaced by someone who can. Am I correct on this?

While in my high school days I knew a fellow student who by rights should have graduated three years ahead of me. Instead, he was pushed through the system and graduated two years ahead of me. I know he was pushed through because I was in a Tenth Grade English Class with him and sat next to him. We each had to read out loud a paragraph in a book the class was studying at the time. When it came to his turn to read, he kept his right index finger under each word as he sounded that word out and I tried to help him sound out the difficult words. He had paused on the word "it", and for that brief moment as he tried desperately to sound it out, the class started to snicker and laugh at him until I helped him with that word. He graduated that summer. When he was out of school he usually worked low paying grunt work and even tried his hand at male exotic dancing. I don't know what has become of him, but the fact is he was pushed through high school because the school system failed to do what it takes to teach him!

Now, my good friend the plumber told me of a story of his confrontation with his children's teachers, where he had received a letter from his oldest son's fourth grade teacher. He even let me read the letter that was sent to him and it did seem like the teacher was informing him to either completely help his child with their homework or else home school his child. My friend had a meeting after school with the young teacher and politely told her that he didn't go to school to be a teacher, he went to school to be a plumber. He didn't expect her to do her own plumbing and she shouldn't expect for him to read his child's school books to be able to help him with his homework at night. He pointed out the fact that she went to school to be a teacher and it is her responsibility for her to do her job, even if it meant that some students may need extra help after classes are over.

Again, when his oldest and middle sons were in high school he was told that both were struggling with their classes. He had arranged a separate meeting with the teachers and guidance councilors for each of his sons. He politely listened to what each teacher had to say and after the teachers and guidance councilors were through speaking my friend asked the teachers if his son were to stay after class and/or school would they be willing to help them with their studies for that particular class. Only one teacher refused, but if too many refused, then my friend would have proposed the same demand that he used on his oldest son's fourth grade teacher. "Do your job you are paid to do and I will do the job I am paid to do!" By being asked as a group the teachers basically couldn't refuse a request like that. An issue could have been brought up at a school board meeting and out into the local newspaper and the argument could get very ugly.

Now don't get me wrong about my point of view of teachers. We as parents are basically pawning off the academic schooling of our children onto a group of people who went to college to do just that. It is not an easy task to do so at times, either. They didn't go to school to be babysitters and we as parents shouldn't expect them to be. Though some students are easily taught, some students are disruptive. Still, teachers should be held accountable for their job of teaching their students soundly as well as parents of the disruptive students should be held accountable for their children's misbehavior. Parents of a child that is disruptive in class should have detention after school along with their disruptive child. They raised their child to be disruptive. That rudeness came from somewhere. Parents should be held accountable as well. What is fair is fair!

There are some teachers that earn their pay and there are some who don't. Some teachers are under paid and there are those who are way too much over paid. Some of this I blame the Teachers' Union for and some I blame the School Committee for by not being responsible enough for holding anyone accountable in justifying the spending of our children's education! We as parents and taxpayers that fund our school systems are putting our children in the hands of professionals to teach them what they need academically to go fourth in life. We need to have a system in place that's accountable enough that we can depend on. Teachers, School Committees, Administrators, like Doctors are not Gods, and we shouldn't treat them as such. They are no different than you or I and should be held accountable. Do your job correctly and morally or else find another career!

Politics and Kids Sports

THIS ISSUE HERE is one of my pet peeves. With that said, let me illuminate those who are involved and those who are not. Kids' Sports are just that, "Kids' Sports" with the emphasis on "Kids'." Outside of the parents that are usually volunteering their time to coach, the rest of the parents should stay on the side line and root for their child's team, with a vocal acknowledgment to ALL of the players on both teams when they do something correctly and it was a great effort on their part. Again, a reminder that it is a "Kids' Sport" and they do like the praise when earned.

We as parents have well intentions, but we should not get involved with the purpose of placing our own children into the big spotlight by placing them in the best positions. The reasons for not doing this are simple;

1. The child may NOT want to be in the spot light
2. There may be other children on your child's team that are more talented and skilled than yours and deserve the spot light
3. These are usually TEAM sports and the TEAM should be coached as a TEAM to be a TEAM, win or lose

Yes, it is advisable to try to coach to win because the TEAM of KIDS does expect it from you. The hell with the parents and what they think, teach the kids on your team to play by the rules, learn the strategies of the game (what to do in different scenarios) get the kids in shape without killing them, and let them have fun, with emphasis on <u>FUN</u>!

I watched a coach at a kid's minor league baseball game talk to his team before the game started. His little pep talk went over what they had to watch out for from the other team and he reminded the kids of his four rules;

1. No Horsing Around
2. Pay Attention
3. Try As Hard As You Can
4. Have Fun

I watched him calm a flustered nine year old pitcher he had on the mound who was struggling with getting the pitches over the plate. He told the kid to take a deep breath, relax, focus, and smile, and have some fun, that it is only a game of catch. Just throw strikes and if the batter hit the ball, the pitcher's teammates in the field could be more involved in the game and practice what they were taught. The child smiled and threw the next six pitches as strikes and got out of the inning.

I talked to this coach after the game and praised him on his coaching. He told me that he coached because it made him feel good inside when a child made their first hit, their first fly ball catch, scored their first goal, or stopped a goal, made a great play, and when they came onto the side line and their fellow team players all gave that player "high fives" and praise, the smile on that player's face that did such a great thing gave this coach tears of joy in his own eyes and he felt very proud of that player and the team for being a team. That my friend is what coaching should be about. It should never be about Politics, or who is who on the social ladder.

While coaching I had suggested on three occasions at the coaches meeting for the teams' draft, that we should place the top twenty or twenty-five best kids in the order pertaining to their skill levels. Then, let them be selected in that order through the draft proceedings so that the teams would be more even with skilled players. I know that a team with very little skilled players and is losing most or all of their games because of it will not play their best and will not have fun and learn to build their skill level up any higher. When teams are very evenly matched and you have to wait for the final inning, the last whistle, or the last buzzer to find out who wins, then the game is not only exciting for the parents to watch, but is also exciting for the kids to play. A child learns more if they are into the game if the teams are evenly matched.

I have coached against other parents who kept their twelve year olds out of Little League and in Minor League Baseball just to stack a team to win a championship. I have coached against parents who had not only their two children, but their nephews and nieces on their team "Locked in and protected" from the start before the draft could begin. All in all they basically had in protected players half of the top ten kids.

My own son was a good soccer player. He was a very tenacious Halfback and when the ball was in his area he was on the ball handler like "flies on shit" and that ball handler had to get rid of the ball or he would lose it to my son. I've watched him and all of the other kids play throughout their Grammar School and Junior High days. I knew who was skilled and who was not so skilled. My son made the High School JV soccer team but failed to make it his sophomore year. Instead, he was replaced by several freshmen that were not as talented, but their parents were in the social clicks.

I had to watch in agony as my son's emotional state of mind deteriorated so bad that he wanted to change schools. Even his own ex-teammates couldn't believe he had gotten cut and replaced with very much less skilled players. The soccer coach in question was a bit arrogant and all I can say is that it just proves the reason why they couldn't get into any championships, or even close to one because of his coaching abilities. This coach even placed players in positions of importance on the field that technically, they were not qualified for, and it was all because their parents were in these special clicks. The players that should have been in those positions were in other positions that didn't take advantage of their best skills.

So you see, politics in kids' sports only hurts the kids and does not help them. Parents involved in these politics can only blame themselves when their High School Teams don't make it to the playoffs and their children don't get recognized.

The Death Penalty

WHAT I AM about to say may or may not piss anyone off, but I'm sure it will. I have thought about this subject over and over and I can not come up with any other way to look at it except as such; death by anyone else's hands in a non defensive posture is still murder. In combat, it not only is self preservation, but it is war and it is necessary. I may disagree with some of the wars that have been fought or are now on going, but they are necessary in order to keep the human population from getting too large too fast. We have killed off or taken away the threat from our own natural predatory enemies. Our only threat to our specie is ourselves. Without child creation and birth control and limits of one child per woman in her life time, and without anymore wars, we as the human specie will overpopulate our planet and completely use up our worlds natural resources, thus, destroying our only place to live. If you do not agree and believe this then you are living in your own fantasy world and you really need a reality check.

It is an awful tragedy when someone takes another human being's life out of greed, hate, or just plain anger. I am also including in this crime the causing of a loss of life even if it wasn't physically from another's hands, rather the cause of which was set fourth by the theft of the victim's personal belongings or emotional belongings such as a loved one.

The states that have the Death Penalty in their laws have pretty clear criteria in their court systems that have to be met in order to follow through with it. There are only a few that do not and have a slightly vague set of rules to go by, which is why a few of their judgments have been overturned recently. To me there would have to be absolute proof that a heinous murder was committed and I mean absolute proof without any shadow of doubt what so ever.

My feeling is that if per chance the wrong person was sentenced and put to death, then those that convicted that unfortunate person, such as a Judge, District Attorney, Assistant District Attorney, and possibly the jurists themselves should as well be facing a murder trial. They took an innocent person's life. They are no different than if they drew a loaded and ready firearm, pointed it at that innocent person and pulled the trigger, and killing that innocent person! The taking of an innocent person's life is still murder. If a drunk driver can be charged for reckless homicide and sentenced to prison, then what the hell is the difference?

When a person is convicted of murder and they are sentenced to death, the person or persons actually taking the convicted person's life away are also guilty of murder as well. Think about it, a death has occurred by an act that did not involve self preservation or an act of war. It is still murder and there is no excuse for it. It doesn't matter if it were the prison guards strapping the convicted person's hands, and body down and flipping the electrical switch on to electrocute him or her, or the doctor that gave the convicted, the lethal injection, or the person opening up the lethal gas valve, it is still taking a human life without the need for self preservation or during an act of war. The taking of a life in this manner is still murder and it can not be excused.

If the death penalty is justified and called for, then it should be the victim's own family that should be the ones that pull the switch, turn the gas valve on, or give the lethal injection. They were the ones who have emotionally lost and should require justice. If the accused is truly guilty then it should be up to the victim's loved ones to ask for the death penalty and it should be them who get justification. If they choose not to take the guilty party's life, then no death penalty should be sought for.

We as a society look up to our individually chosen God for wisdom and enlightenment. It is acknowledged in most every religion that there is only one God for that religion and no others. If this Government on the National as well as the State level acknowledges its belief in a God then why do they practice acting like a God when they preach that there is only one God? To take a life outside of self preservation is preached over and over again to be only done by the hand of God and none other! Any other reason for taking a life is murder, plain and simple. To take a life outside of self preservation is playing God and this is no excuse in my book and I'm God Damn Tired of people playing God!

Was 911 The Truth or Conspiracy?

I WILL ADMIT that I am a very untrusting person when it comes to our Government, and my mistrust is completely justified. It seems to me that since day one of the inception of our Great Nation, that we as a people of the United States of America and as well as of the people of this great world as well, have been lied to almost every step of the way! Whenever there is a very tragic event that involves our Government, politically, strategically, or personally, someone is going to ask "Why did it happen?" With that, all possible scenarios will be thought of and worked out by some of us to see if they are at all feasible.

Take for instance Area 51 and the whole UFO and Outer Space Alien situation. Our Government should come clean with all of it. If Area 51 is only a testing facility for developmental weapon technology, then say so and quit hiding behind the wall of "National Security" and "Rumored UFO Sightings". This country is not a Socialistic State and we are not under a Military Dictatorship either! If all of this is to cover up the truth that Aliens from another world do exist and have been visiting our planet, again, don't hide behind the wall of National Security! If this Government, or any other Government for that matter, is developing weapon technology from the access to Alien Technology, then its time to stop it and cut the crap and come clean with this information. We already have enough ways to destroy our planet without finding out newer ways!

Personally, I am not a hundred percent positive that Aliens from another world and long distance space travel is feasible, but I wouldn't be surprised if it were actually true or even not so true. I do know that our Government has got to stop telling lies to its people. Again, I have to ask if you truly believe that we are free!

JFK's assassination was more than a conspiracy it was a bungled affair from day one! Now I have to ask that all important question, "Who had the most to gain by JFK's death?" Certainly the Vice President, LBJ, and it was stated that he felt like his hands were tied as the Vice President, and that President Kennedy kept him in check that way, giving Bobby Kennedy more power as Attorney General.

The Soviet Union didn't like having their bluff called in Cuba with the Missile Crisis. They could have wanted him killed to keep him from attempting an invasion of Cuba again. A third candidate could be from those that actually run our Government, the ones who put JFK in the Oval Office to start with and since JFK was considered to be a little arrogant, reckless, and a bit of a loose cannon, the affair with Marilyn Monroe, the Bay of Pigs Invasion, and a "Gun Ho" attitude by tripling the combat troops in Viet Nam.

These all could be good enough reasons, except the Soviets would have known that Lyndon Johnson would have done with the Presidency, what he actually did. If the Soviets were involved they would have continued setting up shop in Cuba, which they didn't do. So, therefore that rules out the Soviets, despite Oswald training there in Russia previous to Kennedy's assassination. That would also rule out Oswald and his links to the Soviets. That still doesn't rule out Oswald as the shooter or at least one of the shooters.

Now you have to ask why Oswald would pick an Italian Carcano Carbine for a sniper's weapon. It is a front line weapon of the World War One era. It was designed to knock down the front combatants of a charging army. The bullet's weight and muzzle velocity would probably pass through its first victim and possibly its second if in close proximity, and badly wounding a third if possible. If Oswald had a reloading press and reloaded his own rounds with slightly lighter and jacketed hollow points, it might have helped with the accuracy, but there wasn't any mention that he did this. He probably bought the gun from a surplus gun dealer and therefore bought the factory loaded rounds meant for front line military use. These bullets were made to penetrate, break through bones and proceed onward to the next victim, leaving victims with large, bleeding wounds, with the exit hole about the same size as the entry hole. A gun designed for the front line of the infantry does not have to be accurate to shoot at a mass of bodies coming at you. The idea is to point it at the group of combatants, keep pulling the trigger until the magazine is empty, reload again and again until you are out of ammo, and wound or kill as many as you can without worrying about precise aiming. Plain and simple, the Carcano Carbine is not a sniper weapon!

Now I have viewed the JFK assassination video several times and the second shot, the head shot, shows the President's right, front, top of his head exploding out and up. This suggests that;

1. a jacketed hollow point was used for maximum killing effect, meaning if the entry wound was any place from the lower part of the rib cage and up, the exit wound would indeed explode out and cause lethal damage
2. the shot had to be more on the level and not starting from a point fifty to sixty feet higher (sixth floor of the book depository, ten feet per floor average) than President Kennedy's limousine, which gives the elevation of a thirty-five to sixty degree angle, which is too much of a downward angle to cause JFK's head to explode upward as the video shows.

Wrong gun, wrong ammunition, and wrong angle, and add to the fact that Oswald barely qualified to be a sharp shooter in the Marines makes it very unlikely that he killed the President.

Now the "Magic Bullet Theory" is definitely a controversy and whoever believes this as the truth to what happened is a very dumb and gullible person and I can't believe that anyone is that truly stupid. I will conceive that the Carcano round is designed to penetrate and exit mostly intact with a little mushrooming effect if encountering any bone, but the weight and muzzle velocity added to the fact that it was supposedly shot in a downward trajectory giving less velocity slow down, this bullet would not have been deflected to the degree that it was suggested. There had to be more than one shooter and possibly they were using true sniper rifles with scopes and silencers and sniper rounds, soft tips to jacketed hollow points.

Oswald's gun was probably fired three times by someone and not necessarily by Oswald. One of the rounds could have hit someone in the motorcade, but if I were a betting man, my bets would be on someone on the second floor of the book depository, or at least in the near level and vicinity because of the angle the second round that exploded the Presidents head had to be. There were other shooters as well and because of the angle and positions of the wounds to Governor John Connally and by the testimony from the spectators, there had to be snipers near the grassy knoll and possibly on the other side of the motorcade as well.

There have been a few so called "Experts" to discount the conspiracy theories, from CIA and FBI Agents following Oswald around the previous year or two, to computer experts with simulated tactics that the magic bullet is viable. There are plain and simple facts there, and common sense along with the facts, and the question of "If a conspiracy or not, who had the most to gain by this act?"

The killing of Oswald by Jack Ruby suggests that there were possible Organized Crime involvement as well, and that may be true, but why would they possibly pay Oswald to kill the President and use Ruby to kill Oswald? It doesn't make any sense at all.

Organized Crime walks hand in hand with the Feds and I have seen it. The mob gives the Feds a bone every now and then to make it appear that they are accomplishing something. Back in the early Sixties there wasn't the Terrorist Threats, or Gang Violence, or the Drug Trafficking we have today. The Feds wouldn't have anything to justify their existence if there weren't any organized crime syndicates then and that is why the small time "wanna' be's" were served up as bones to be chewed.

Did Ruby kill Oswald because he was so overwhelmed with emotion over the death of a President he admired and honored? I don't believe that at all. Whether Oswald did it or not he fits a certain profile as well as does Ruby as a deep cover agent. Let's face it, there are at least twice as many Government agencies that are a secret to the American People than there are the ones that are known. It wasn't until the past thirty years that the National Security Agency became more familiarly known and an almost household name. Until then no one ever heard of them or knew that they existed.

If Oswald was a deep cover agent it explains the defection to Russia and the hesitation by them to take him into their confidence. It would explain the same with Cuba and the day to day whereabouts of Oswald that were given to the news media are very easily planted, especially back then when people were quite dumb and trusting.

Ruby fits the deep cover profile as well. He owned a Night Club and somewhere he probably had some connections with organized crime, which made him the Feds' inside man and expendable. Ruby was probably ordered to kill Oswald and was told he would not be convicted. When he was, he was probably told to take the punishment or end up like Oswald. Use Oswald as a scapegoat, have Ruby kill Oswald, two or more snipers to make sure the President was killed, it sounds like a perfectly planned operation, even a military one!

If you are wondering why I believe this scenario, then think about all of the major players of the government that were involved in the investigation and so therefore the Government had to be involved in the cover up. They had to get rid of a president that wasn't playing by their rules and they had to squash the idea of any cover up.

The Ohio State incident where the National Guard was ordered to break up the anti Vietnam War protest there and four students were shot by the National Guard is another incident that proves my point. This is just another example to how far a Government will go to eliminate threats to its way of thinking and its way of running the world! Give someone who's angry something to pacify them for awhile and sooner or later they'll forget why they are angry. Let them get back to their comfort zone and the problem will disappear.

I knew a gentleman who worked for a paper mill back in 1974. In July of that year the mill workers' union voted to not take the company's offer and they went on strike for two months. The mill owners and corporate executives knew that they only had to wait the workers out two or three months and they would accept any terms to come back to work. It only took two months and the workers accepted an offer that was less than was originally offered. Again, when a person finds themselves out of their comfort zone they will do anything to get back into it again!

The Moon Landing in my beliefs actually did happen. I have seen the conspiracy side of it, but it doesn't convince me enough to believe in it. I will say that there might have been more dangerous situations that had occurred during the many various space missions that the general public was never made aware of.

Don't even get me started about O J's trial. I know for a fact that fresh blood, even at freezing temperatures will dry on your skin in less than five minutes. O J's ex was a coke queen and Goldman was along for the coke ride, along with what coke queens do best. O J helped the sports' gambling by giving them insider info, and he decided he wanted out of all of it, but his ex didn't. She liked the snorting and the partying. Someone else had a different plan and sent a message. Connect the dots unless you are stupid.

My thoughts on 911 might piss off a lot of people. I tip my hats to the Fire Fighters and Police Officers who did their job and then some. I tip my hat to all of those who risked their lives in those two buildings and the adjacent ones with trying to help get people out of harms way and to try to find survivors in the aftermath. In the face of tragedy humans can put away their differences and pull together to help those in need.

Now let me remind you that ALL Major Governments have "Think Tanks", or groups of very intelligent people whose sole purpose is to think of scenarios of every possible tragedy and how to solve the problem. With that said, our Government knew since the sixties that a large jet plane half filled with fuel could become a very lethal weapon in a very populated area! Have you ever seen Napalm hit the ground from a jet fighter bomber? It is not rocket science to make the connection.

I have viewed the conspiracy videos and heard the pros and cons of these conspiracies. One of our own Government's protocols is that in the event of deciding the life of a few over the lives of many, the termination of the lives of a few will always take precedent! To prove my point, when it comes to dealing with Hijackers, the American Government has made it very clear that we "Do Not" make deals with them. This basically means that the few Hostages that might be on a bus, boat, train or plane are expendable, collateral damage. If the Hijack is taken out by a missile, then the many were spared.

Those four jet airliners would have been destroyed in flight shortly after it was determined that they had been hijacked and changing course towards any major city in the United States, especially if their flight direction coarse change had them heading in a direction towards Washington D.C. The order to termination of these jet airliners would have been given and there would only be collateral damage outside of New York City and Washington DC and not the damage to the Twin Towers and the Pentagon, Especially after the first jet hit the Twin Towers.

Another protocol is that in the event of any suspected terroristic attack in the United States while the President is in the country, he is supposed to be <u>immediately</u> taken to a secure location. He was in a grammar school classroom and was only told about the attack and was not hustled off right away to his secure location until some time after. This only proves that the Secret Service knew he was never in any danger.

This brings several questions in mind.

1. If the President was never in any danger, then how did they know there wasn't a fifth jet airliner controlled by terrorists on route to where the President was?

2. If the Air Force didn't follow protocol and shoot down the first jet airliner that hit the World Trade Center, why <u>didn't</u> they on the second one? They had plenty of time to do so and they had Fighter Jets already scrambled and waiting.

3. Why <u>didn't</u> the Air Force follow protocol on the one that hit the Pentagon?

4. Why <u>didn't</u> they follow protocol on the one that the passengers took down in a rural part of Pennsylvania?

5. How could the CIA, the FBI, the NSA, and all of the other agencies of the United States Government <u>lose sight</u> of nineteen suspected terrorists? They followed most of them for a few months around the world and then they lose them just before the supposed attack?

Since World War Two and the attack on Pearl Harbor there was an agreement that the world powers would not participate in any form of assassinations. With that said, it has been an accepted assumption that we use covert missions to "take out" any suspected individuals whom plot against the United States, especially in a terroristic plot involved in doing the kind of damage that was done on 911.

This means that with the information that a jet airliner half full of fuel is a serious weapon, that there were known terrorists taking flight lessons, that they were spending a lot of money having a good time a few days before the 911 attacks, there was enough evidence to enact the protocol to either abduct them secretly or take them out permanently. Why weren't they assassinated? The FBI, the CIA, NSA, and all other agencies report to their directors and in turn, their directors report to the Chief of Staffs along with the President and some of his cabinet. I find it very unlikely that any of this information was ever withheld from the channels of progression. If this government still insists that they bungled the intelligence side of this tragedy, then they all should have been fired, impeached, or imprisoned for being that stupid!

Our Government went through Impeachment Proceedings of our current President of the time for getting a blow job in the White House. Tell me why the Administration that got us into this great big mess never even came close to an impeachment? It is because "We the People" do not run our country. We are a flock of sheep that are too scared to get out of our precious comfort zone. So, tell me, are we free?

I've heard the argument that there was no communication between the various agencies and that was why the 911 attacks occurred. Our Government operates on a set of rules, checks and balances as you might call it. They do not change with each administration and are there to ensure that the United States remains safe and business goes on as usual. Protocols are in place for a reason and are always followed, just as the Secret Service quickly cover up and protect the President in case of immediate danger, just as our nuclear arsenal will be readied and launched upon any nuclear threat from our adversaries.

Protocols are there for a reason and are practiced and followed to the dot of a period for that reason. If anyone tells you different then we have the most stupid leaders running our country in the whole world, and I truly find that is very hard to believe! I can not believe that we have a leadership that is more arrogant and more gullible than the American People! That our heads of state fell asleep at the wheel and let over 3,000 people die on American soil is so unbelievable I am beside myself.

Now, how would you pacify an angry nation of Americans if it was realized that their leaders had fallen asleep at the wheel? Before they started to suspect any wrong doing, shift their growing anger towards a much better and believable enemy, like Bin Laden and al-Qaeda and/or Saddam Hussein, weapons of mass destruction. Again, why did this happen, how did it happen, and who had the most to gain by it all? I know one very big corporation that had a whole lot of to gain and already had one of their own in the right places of power to see to it!

The news media had reported awhile before the 911 attacks that the newly elected President commented that his father was threatened by Saddam Hussein with an attempted and failed assassination, and that he, the President of the United States was not going to let him get away with it. Take into consideration that both the President and the Vice President had close ties to the oil industry and that Iraq was in the middle of one of the largest oil deposits in the world, and all was needed was a reason to invade Iraq and plunder its resources. That my friend is <u>Who</u> had <u>What</u> to gain, and <u>Why</u>!

If you remember my lesson on our Revolutionary War and how the common man was talked into fighting against the British with scare tactics, then you see how we, the American People were coerced into the Iraqi war. We were told that Saddam had compiled an arsenal of "Weapons of Mass Destruction" and he was allowing al-Qaeda to operate terrorist training camps inside of Iraq. This whole idea that the Iraqi leader was doing such bad things against us was made so believable by preaching it to us over and over again and again that we, as the American People believed it all and wanted Saddam and his family of cut throats out of power and blown up, hung and quartered. After the 911 attacks it all became so believable that the American People wanted blood. So filled with rage they couldn't see the truth from the lies.

Now can anyone tell me about all this so called "evidence" that Saddam had weapons of mass destruction and where it came from and why we didn't actually find any? Can you tell me why no one was ever held accountable for the invasion of a country under false pretences? Can anyone tell me why we made a nation suffer severely with our invasion and occupation while a selected few of our own oil industry took control of the oil there? These selected few solely supplied, transported, and purchased at a very low rate the Iraqi oil. Sounds like what organized crime syndicates do here in the United States with area restaurants, grocers, night clubs, and the likes by strong arming them into purchasing what they will supply these establishments with to conduct business.

We started war by invading Afghanistan, and shortly afterwards we invaded Iraq. We moved some of the military forces out of Afghanistan and deployed them to Iraq, which spread us too thin in Afghanistan and that is why we hadn't captured or killed Osama Bin Laden for more than eight years, and why we are still fighting a bloody war there to this day. The real threat was inside of Afghanistan and not in Iraq, which was where Al-Qaeda had their training camps and where Bin Laden was hiding. We new this for a fact and had true documentation on this.

We should have used all of our troops to finish the war there before starting one with Iraq. We had the satellite pictures as proof of evidence to use to missile attack and destroy these so called Weapons of Mass Destruction. We didn't need any approval to missile attack Afghanistan before the 911 attacks, so we didn't need any approval after the 911 attacks to launch missiles at Iraq. This is not hindsight this is basic common sense, especially after the Russians had failed to conquer Afghanistan a few years earlier. It seems to me that our own Government acted with very much stupidity and "We the People" are no better for allowing it.

What is this I hear you say? We did not have a say in going to war over there? Our Congress, Senate, the President and Vice President decided on it for us. So I ask you again, "Are We Free?" "Who had the most to gain by this action?" "Where was the great and all powerful United Nations in all of this?

Without the 911 attacks there wouldn't be a reason to invade Iraq. This is a simple plain and honest fact. That is why I find it very hard to believe that what the American People and the rest of the world were told about it is not the truth! Our Government and all of its policies and all of its protocols are there in place to NOT allow anything like this to ever happen. Our elected government is not that stupid and if they hide behind their stupidity, then it is time for "We the People" to stand up and take back our country and rewrite the rules! So tell me, why wasn't anyone held accountable? I'll tell you why. It is because "We the People" are as stupid as they say we are and can not think or act for ourselves. We are a nation of sheep and we need them to herd us in the right direction! A plain and simple fact of our life!

"Where was the great and all powerful United Nations in all of this? They were sitting on their pampas asses and doing nothing. This was an organization that was supposed to not allow tyranny and human injustice to go on around the world. What the hell good are they if they can not do their job that they are paid to do? Why they are not held accountable as well? Who is supposed to hold them as such?

My Thoughts On Aids

Now THIS IS a subject that I know that what I have to say about it is going to really upset someone. I really don't mean to and yes, my heart very much goes out to those that contracted it unknowingly or collaterally. Aids are a very nasty disease that is not particular who its victims are. It is not a Gay disease, it is not a Blacks' disease, and it is not a disease sent from hell by a God to punish the unfaithful. I find it very hard to believe that African monkeys gave Aids to the world. My personal beliefs are that Aids was designed by Man's own hands and the African population in that region where it was first diagnosed as a disease was the way to find out if it would work to its design!

It is believed that the disease has been around since the late Nineteenth or early Twentieth Century. If this is so, then think about what was going on during that time period. There were certainly strong prejudices against those of color then, as well as chemical and biological warfare. True Africans were trying to take back their lands from the white conquerors and what better way to test an experimental biological weapon than to test it on a population that a lot of the world's dominating group of people considered inferior. Add to the fact that it was in a rural part of Africa that it first was affecting and there were no White People there to affect. Have I pissed anyone off yet?

Ever since there has been wars fought by vast and organized armies there has been someone trying to invent a way to kill efficiently and on a large scale level. First we had spears and shields. Then along came bows and arrows and catapults. Somewhere along the way someone thought about pouring boiling hot water and oil on attackers, and even oil pits that were lit on fire to burn the attackers as well. Gun powder was invented and primitive guns and cannons changed the battlefield. Gasoline and diesel motors were invented and we developed trucks with machine guns and tanks with mobile artillery. Soon after came planes and jets and choppers with machine guns, bombs, Napalm, and Agent Orange, then rockets and missiles, and nuclear weapons.

Along the way we, as the human race experimented with chemicals that could either render our enemy helpless or cause them death. We even developed biological weapons that would kill a group of people or a village, town, city, or a nation. Some were air born, some by drinking water, and some by bodily fluid contact. We, as a species, raised on fearing a God, have developed into quite the specie. We destroy life around us and we are destroying the world that created us and we will probably destroy ourselves by our own hand. By becoming an intelligent life form, we became the most stupid one that ever existed!

As I've stated, I believe that the Aids Virus was designed by human hands and unleashed on a small population of a remote village of Africans. When it was probably designed, it was probably figured that since it had to be contracted by sexual intercourse or fluid exchange, that if it went beyond the test village, then it would only infect blacks and those who sympathized with blacks. No self respecting white would even care.

Because of the inability to come up with a cure for Aids is the reason I believe this theory. Every other disease that naturally evolves from another form of itself and finds a way to infect the human population, we have found cures for and vaccines to make us immune to it. Aids is the only one we can't and that is why I believe it was man made and thrust upon the human population. Though we have yet to find the cure for the common cold, it is not as deadly as Aids.

Aids primarily infect those that have many sexual lovers and shared needle use. There were a few that contracted it by blood splatter, by passing it on to their expectant child and by nursing a child, but the majority were of sexual encounter and shared needle use. Take into account that the extremely wealthy that inherited their wealth don't mix with the common persons, the very religious consider Aids an act of God to filter out the badly sinned, and you can understand why it has taken research so long to act and come up with something to either cure or help slow it down. Again, I ask all of you overly religious people, if your, "All Powerful God" is so powerful, so forgiving, and so compassionate that why do the newborn get the Aids Virus from their mothers and are condemned to hell?

I've listened to arguments about whether to or not allow children with Aids, go to school with children who don't have the disease. I apologize to those who are going to get offended by my next statement, but what I am about to say isn't of prejudice but of common sense fact. Doctors, Nurses, Emergency Medical Technicians, Law Enforcement Officers, or any other person involved in handling a person that has wounds or bodily fluids being expelled has to wear surgical rubber gloves. If the NBA is so conscious of covering up a wound to allow the wounded player to continue playing, though I don't understand why no other sport follows this policy, then there is a good reason for it.

If contact with blood, spit or saliva can transmit the Aids Virus, then how would you feel if your child got into a physical fight with a child who had Aids, or a child with Aids trying to break up a physical fight between someone and his or her friend? When my children were little I thought about this scenario. If I did nothing and allowed my child to be in the same school as a child with aids, and something happened and my child contracted Aids because of it, I couldn't live with myself for doing this to my child. Could you?

Fortunately I didn't have a scenario like this to contend with, but I strongly am against anyone with aids to attend a public or private school of children who don't have the Aids virus. I remember what school was like with the bullies and the jocks that thought their shit didn't stink and they got away with everything. My own children were raised to walk away, never turn your back, Fight if you don't have a choice, and come to the defense of the innocent. Again, kids are kids, and they are a reflection of their parents. If you are a parent of a child with aids, place yourself in another parent's shoes whose child didn't have Aids. Would you want to take that chance of collateral blood splatter?

Our Soldiers Deserve Better

I HAVE SEEN on the news where there were Veterans' Hospitals that were unfit for animals, let alone humans. Our soldiers who were casualties of war were mistreated and wrongly diagnosed and were basically left to suffer. Many of our Vets have become homeless, wondering the streets of our cities. None of them asked to be treated like this when they were drafted or enlisted. A great many that were wounded have learned to survive and cope with their disabilities. It hurts me very deeply to know that they hurt and for some of them, our government has turned its back on them.

Yes, there are a few that might try to capitalize on their misfortunes, but I don't think that there are all that many, for so many to be left out in the cold. Not everyone can be a soldier and handle the physical and mental state a soldier has to be in. Unless from birth you grow up inside a war zone, life in the United States doesn't prepare you enough for combat. Very few can turn it on and off like a light switch, and it will be with you for life, make no mistake about it.

I can tell a soldier that has seen very little combat and the ones who were in the deep shit. Those are the ones that keep it all to their selves. They are the ones that suffer the nightmares that never really go away. If a person gives their life to the armed forces, whether it is for only three years or for twenty, whether they have been wounded or not, our government should never, ever turn its back on them. They put their life on the line when they were ordered to and they should be treated better than any civilian. The government owes them at least that.

This little paragraph is for those in command of the military. Like a big corporation, our military is run. Certain losses are expected and accepted, and the same with collateral damage. A mission is designed to be achieved and sometimes it doesn't turn out that way. Like in big corporations there are those, that no matter how well oiled a machine is and how well it is operating, it only takes one asshole to screw it up. Unfortunately I am not allowed to mention certain individuals or certain incidences that I am thinking about at this moment, but the cover up that takes place in the aftermath is a load of bull. My point in this matter was covered earlier with the Death Penalty. It just pisses me off to no extent that certain military officers get away with it and the poor grunts suffer the consequences for following orders.

I knew a friend that used to play guitar and sing in night clubs on occasion. He had written a few songs and would play them, mixing them in a set of other songs written by others. One time, he had finished a set with a song he had written, but never played in public before, titled; "Jesus Christ, Who the Hell Are You". It was a ballad of a young man growing up in a sheltered life style in a very rural part of the country. He had left home at age eighteen and entered a big city. He was lured into an Army recruiting office and he signed his name. The story in the song is told by another and it tells about life in the military, a soldier's point of view.

It is a very moving ballad and when my friend finished the song and the set, he was greeted by half of the patrons giving him a standing ovation. As he walked through the crowd towards the bar, he was asked by a couple of men to join them at their table. He noticed that one of them had tears streaming out of his eyes and down his cheeks. The two men were sort of "Hippy" looking with slightly long hair and medium length beards.

When he sat down at their table with them, they asked him about the song, and both men thanked him for writing a song about a soldier's point of view. A couple of weeks later when my friend played in that night club again, he was asked to play that song again at the end of his set. He did and again, received a standing ovation. He told me he allowed himself to get fully involved in the flow of the song, and he felt his own throat start to choke a little as his own tears flowed out of his closed eyes during the last verse. He could tell that at least a quarter of the fifty or sixty people crowding the little night club that night were Vietnam Vets, and again, he received a standing ovation.

More Local Gripes

I'M SURE ALL of you have seen the traffic lights turn yellow and with in three seconds they turn red and motorists are still going threw the intersection and through the red light. You've probably noticed that even though you are actually going the speed limit, your traffic light turns yellow and the only way you can stop before or even at the stop line, you would have to practically lock your brakes up.

Take into consideration that there might be someone behind you not prepared to stop that quickly and you could have an accident. If you were not paying strict attention to the stop light, you will be going through the red light. You try to pay attention to it, to catch it when it changes from green to yellow, so you can hit your breaks quickly, but something usually diverts your attention for that very short moment. It could be a pedestrian picking their way through traffic in trying to cross the road, legally or illegally. Sometimes it's the car in front of you or beside you that is trying to force their way into your lane.

At an average traffic lighted intersection with a speed limit of 30 mph an average passenger vehicle is covering 44 feet per second. In the 3 seconds the traffic light stays yellow for, this vehicle will cover 132 feet. Given it takes at least a second for reaction time, the driver has 2 seconds to stop the vehicle doing 30 mph with in 88 feet, and not have the car behind them smash into the rear of their vehicle.

How many times have you been sitting there in your vehicle, stopped at a red light, and the light for your flow of traffic turned green, but you can't go, not until everyone finishes going through their red lights, crossing your traffic lane. It's not just the civilian traffic, but I have seen on several occasions a local police car drive right on through a red light. They didn't even have their lights flashing, though I have seen them turn them on long enough for them to get through the intersection, just to pull into the local doughnut shop or fast food joint. This isn't even a joke. I'm sure some of you have seen it or have done it.

Not to piss off the Police, because I have the utmost respect for them and the job they have to do, but I do have a pet peeve on something they do, or not do, which is the case here. Our once, great Governor Dukakis passed a law to have only Police Officers direct traffic along the road whenever there was any road construction or telephone or electric wire repair going on. The Police Union insisted on a very high wage for their officers to receive for this job. Later on the law was amended to include anyone who had so many hours in traffic control training, though they wouldn't get the high pay for it.

Now I was being sarcastic by giving the governor any praise. My pet peeve is that, yes, it can be very dangerous for someone to be standing to the side of traffic in trying to control it. I don't feel however that they should be paid such high wages for it. Ask any Police Officer in Massachusetts if it's a gravy job or not and they'll grab all of the gravy they can.

My other pet peeve is driving through a road construction site and seeing a Police Officer on his cell phone gabbing away for the twenty minutes I have to wait there until the single lane of traffic can proceed forward. An hour later after I have done my shopping and am passing through the construction site again and it seems he is still on the phone. He is supposed to be paying attention to the traffic and controlling it, and paying attention to the construction workers and their vehicles to keep them out of harm's way.

Then you have the Police Officer who is more fascinated in the movements of the excavator rather than the traffic that almost hit each other head on, because one of them is trying to avoid a pot hole at thirty-five miles per hour. Then there's the Police Officer bullshitting for a half an hour with one of the construction workers leaning on a shovel. I will admit that the majority of the Police Officers directing traffic on construction sites usually are doing their job exactly how it should be done, but its not fair to us tax payers to have some of our programs cut by the local government and by the state as well, and pay high wages to a Police Officer who can't do a simple job right. If some of the waste spending was reined in then some of our necessary programs wouldn't need to be cut.

Another good example is watching a state highway worker using a state highway pickup truck on a Sunday, picking up sheet rock at the local Home Depot. There are perks and there are wasteful perks. Like some of our governmental employees' families with government licensed gas guzzling, large Sport Utility Vehicles. I don't mind my tax dollars going towards transportation for certain members' families' personal use, but unless they live in a very rural area they can get along with a front wheel drive economy car or else buy their own vehicle and pay for their own fuel!

There are times when I often wondered about how much money is really collected through property taxes, excise taxes, and the likes, and how much is really paid out to keep a town or city operating. Then I think about programs in schools getting cut, how bad the roads are and how half ass they get repaired, and how many wasteful perks there are in all of this mess. It's a shame there is no accountability anymore in the world. It's a real shame. It makes you wonder how many people have their hands in the till or are getting paid way too much for the job that they are actually doing.

Since I'm venting out my frustration, I have one more thing to mention. In Massachusetts we have a pedestrian crossing walk law. If a pedestrian steps off of the curb in this designated crossing walk, traffic is supposed to stop and let them cross the road. Now it is my understanding that if the crossing walk is at a traffic stop light and therefore the pedestrian also has a crossing light, then the pedestrian has to wait for the light to stop all traffic and indicate that it is their turn to cross. If a pedestrian crosses without waiting for the light to change or crosses the road outside of a designated crossing walk, traffic doesn't have to stop right there to let them cross. What upsets me the most are the pedestrians who "Jay Walk" and get pissed at you when you don't stop and let them cross the road. Especially the ones who are too lazy to walk ten feet over to actually get into a designated crossing walk. Personally, and of coarse jokingly, there should be an open season on Jay Walkers. Just kidding, but seriously, just kidding.

How to solve the Problems
In the Middle East

I HAVE TRAVELED there briefly and have had many friends from there throughout my past. It is and always will be a crossroad in the world, geographically, economically, religiously, politically. It is one of the few places where humans began civilization. It was a crossroad for trade between Europe, Africa, and Asia. Wars were fought there for the same four reasons. As time went past, everyone else seemed to stick there nose into the affairs there, wanting to be the deciding factor to what would take place there.

In my eyes it wasn't fair to the Palestinians to lose there land in such fashion, but the Jewish People also deserve to have their own land. My Grandmother use to tell me not to cry over spilled milk. So, I look at this and can only say that the past is just that, the past. It should be left there. Nothing was perfect then, no one was. We as Humans became the dominant specie for a reason, though some of the reasons were not our finest hour, but we were able to evolve and learn from some of our mistakes.

It is about time people of the Middle East put away their differences. Israel is there and it would probably take a nuclear war to change that, and that would be the most <u>STUPID</u> way of handling the situation that could ever be.

Personally, <u>ALL</u> nuclear weapons should be dismantled and destroyed. Any form of a weapon of that much mass destruction should never be allowed to be owned, developed, or used in any way, shape, or form. For the life of me I can not understand why the human race needs to destroy our very own world, and for what, to keep someone else from taking our homes, our way of living, our way of life away? If we as humans are this selfish, this terrible, then why don't we develop a disease that only kills humans and let's end our reign here on Earth without destroying the very planet that created and nurtured us.

Someone needs to take the initiative and ban all nuclear weapons and every other weapon of mass destruction, and I don't mean have it done in twenty or so years from now, I mean within five years or less. Our children can't wait that long.

As far as the Middle East, Israel should stop expanding and settling any land that is not in its exact and worldly recognized boundaries. The Palestinians should be able to keep the West Bank and the Gaza Strip, let them be recognized by the world as a free and democratic nation. Egypt should give to the Palestinian people some of there land, they can afford it, as well as Jordan should do the same.

I grew up in a rural part of my state. It seemed that everyone knew everyone. You always took the initiative to lend a neighbor a hand without waiting to be asked. That was the way my parents grew up and my Grandparents as well. It shouldn't take a serious catastrophe to bring Nations together. It takes a simple initiative to step forward and lend a helping hand with no strings attached. And for the one receiving the helping hand, they should also lend their hand out with no strings attached. How hard is that? The past is just that, the past.

I think it would be great to see Israel either pull its settlers out of the Gaza Strip and the West Bank, or consent to an agreement that those Israelis that chose not to give up their homes in both areas would become Resident Aliens of Palestine with permanent Green Cards. These Israelis would and should be protected by the Palestinian Government as if they were Palestinian Citizens. The same goes for Palestinians living in Israel.

Israel could offer to help the Palestinians with road building, with agriculture, and anything else they could offer. Palestine could do the same as well. When neighbors help each other out it builds a very strong community! It also sets an example for surrounding communities, and Nations to follow! Look what is happening now to the Middle East.

The Egyptian People stood up for themselves and voiced their opinion with pretty much peaceful public protesting. President Hosni Mubarak and his cabinet stepped down and hopefully the Egyptian Military allows free elections as their people demanded. I hope it works out for them. All people of every nation should be allowed to live their life as free, peaceful citizens. To have the power to choose their government and the power to make a majority decision on the laws their government wants to pass of what affects their lives.

My heart and all of my hope goes out to the Egyptian People and to the other Nations' Peoples that are trying to do what the Egyptian People have done. Don't give up, stay determined, keep unified and all voice out as one and you will overcome the tyranny that has ruled you for so long. May the American People also sit up and take notice. And by the way, where is the United Nations in all of this, as the tyranny continues to take place in Syria, Libya, Yemen, and other Arab worlds. Sounds to me like that the UN is sitting on their hands and letting the Arab World destroy its self.

As I have stated before, all people need to be free. Free from tyranny, from injustice, from prejudice, from genocide, free from dictatorship, free to voice their opinion, free to make their own decisions on how to live their lives. Again, I say to the United Nations and to the world, "shit or get off the pot!" Lend a helping hand. Think about it, a truly free world, what a concept.

The Black Gold We Call Oil

EVER SINCE THE first combustion engine was manufactured, we the common people of the world have been at crude oil's mercy. Like cancer, crude oil has polluted and destroyed our lives as well as our planet. There is no other natural resource that has been so manipulated and controlled by the wealthiest, and forced down the throats of the rest of us. Gold, silver, and diamonds are far too rare to be exploited in the same way. Like addictive narcotics, crude oil has the human race badly addicted and no one cares. It is a very huge part of our comfort zone. Remember that thought? Our comfort zone, which is how we live our lives and controls how we say, act, and respond.

The United States had forced most of the Native Americans to reside on reservations in what is now the state of Oklahoma. Then crude oil was discovered there and the reservations were moved to even less favorable areas like Florida and the Dakota Territories, taking away any wealth that the Native Americans could have received from the land that was forced down their throats.

Crude oil is so much apart of our lives that the average person has no idea how many products we use every day that have some form of by-product of crude oil.

Now, have you ever wondered why every time we have a hurricane in the Gulf of Mexico, or any crisis in the Middle East, or any other problem with the drilling, refining, transportation of the stuff that disrupts the process, prices jump and we have to pay the price for it? The cost of fuel at the pumps, heating oil and gasoline, motor oil, air fare, electricity, even the food we buy at the grocery store is affected. Everything we use in our everyday lives, in our comfort zone, is affected. It is all centered around crude oil. The food we eat is transported by truck, by train, by boat, and by plane, and all of these things use some form of petroleum in their engines.

You would think that if a refinery or two went down the other refineries would step up the production process to make sure the oil flows at a steady rate. It would be a safe bet that there are plenty of oil tankers out on the oceans that would be more than enough supply to keep things going at the usual pace until the other refineries got into a higher gear and producing more in the course of a week. My friends, it is a simple matter of why not take advantage of a situation whenever it arises.

Whenever you hear on the news that crude oil stocks are on the rise because of some production distraction and it is the investors speculating that there is going to be a shortage and that is why the price for a barrel of crude oil has risen. Do you try to envision who are the investors? If you own an oil company, chances are you own the majority shares. If you own an automobile manufacturing company, you own a large share of the oil stocks because your product uses it. Large banks and financial institutions are large owners of oil stock because they front the money for oil production. You can have a very safe bet that all of your "Big Business" that run the world own oil companies, own auto manufacturing, and control the price of crude oil.

The Oil Cartels of the Middle East, the American Oil Companies, the British Oil Companies, the Russian Oil Companies, the Dutch Oil Companies all control not only the oil production, but every aspect that depends on crude oil. All of these very huge companies, whether you like it or not control the world. If the average person has to pay extra for a gallon of gasoline, or a higher electric bill or the grocery bill each week gets a little higher and higher, they will complain, but they will accept it because they do not want to fall out of their comfort level! If we the common people are willing to pay the price, then who is to blame?

So tell me, who has the most to gain by the higher crude oil prices, and who has the most to lose? Again, are we free?

With all of the technology that has been developed throughout the years, one would think that we wouldn't need fossil fuels anymore. You would also have to wonder exactly how much of that technology has been suppressed and kept from the general public because it would cut into immensely or even eliminate the need for crude oil. As a common person I feel my hands are not only tied, but I am being forced fed so much crude oil that I actually bleed it out every time I am cut. As an American Citizen my everyday life depends on the flow of crude oil. It feels as if I am a junky and I need my everyday fix of the stuff! If only the common people of the world would band together and demand the world be fossil fuel free, then again, the biggest businesses of the world would own all of that technology too and we all will still be in the same boat.

My Point of View About Government Welfare

I HAVE BEEN a very hard working and honest individual all of my life. I raised my children as such. My parents were raised in the same manner and their parents and grandparents before them. I was raised believing that you never receive something for nothing and shouldn't. Even in gambling there is a price to pay. Unless you are an individual that can fall completely into crap and come out smelling like a rose, it costs you to gamble and win. Gambling is an expensive way to entertain your self.

Yes, sometimes a person or a family can fall on hard times, and there are those that are impoverished. For the average minority that grows up in the projects, the slums, or homeless, society and the world's wealth created your situation. Anyone who disputes this fact has their head up their ass to put it quite frankly. It wasn't fare for that to happen and it is not at all fare to keep anyone repressed into that situation. For a living animal species that claims to be so powerful and so intelligent that they dominate a world of living things, no one should ever be kept down from being an equal!!!

With that said, there is a point to never stop trying and a point to never try enough. In the minds of the wealthy it is a handout to the poor, to help clear a somewhat guilty conscience. To those with their hands out it is a way of life. It is like a company keeping a blind eye to their employees stealing a little from them and the thieving employees feeling they are getting what they feel they deserve from lack of decent pay. If the company shared the wealth a little more then perhaps there wouldn't be a desire to steal. Then again, there are those, rich or poor, that are never satisfied with what they have.

My thought on the Welfare System here in the United States is that if you want something you need to give something in return. For a girl growing up in the projects what does she have to look forward to? If she stays in school and studies hard and keeps her grades up she might be one of the few to actually make a better life for her self. The same goes for a boy as well. The chances for that are very slim. These odds really suck and are hard to accept. It is as bad as going for a job and knowing you are one in a thousand that are going for that one and only job.

Growing up in the projects isn't great, but it has its upside. You have a roof over your head and a working bathroom, hopefully. For those who have a slumlord for a landlord, one who doesn't fix things that are wrong or broken it can be a rough life. My personal point of view is that the slumlord should be shackled and displayed in public wearing a sign describing what they are being punished for. On the same matter those who do not take care of their apartments and/or destroy them should suffer the same consequence. Hold yourself accountable for your actions!

A girl who grows up poor feels she has only one asset, and that is her body. If she is lucky she "hooks" a boy that can make it out of the poverty and into the wealth. It is a natural form of life that is imbedded in the genetic code of most animals, especially in humans. Strength, wealth, higher intelligence are signs of a better chance of survival of the fittest in human society. Just look at how many girls and women chase after Rock n' Rollers, Athletes, successful Actors. They are even willing to have sex with them freely in hope to either get pregnant or become married to them. In probably half the cases it is not for looks, especially in Rock n' Rollers and some Athletes because in my opinion some of these individuals are the ugliest men in the world.

One might think that these girls and women that actively participate in these activities are very much lacking in intelligence. In most cases it may be so, but in all cases it is a natural law of survival. Boys and men are no different.

Girls will get pregnant by using their bodies to entice a boy close enough to get their hooks into them. Boys will lie, cheat, and steal to get a shot of ass from a girl and most of the time to dump her in pursuit for another shot of ass from another girl. Again, it is a natural law of nature. Instead of males facing off with each other for the rights to breed with a certain female or females, humans make themselves more desirable to a female by using lies. It is the human way of life.

In the welfare system when a girl turns a certain age she is no longer under the liability of her mother and is no longer supported by the government. When she is pregnant she falls back under the welfare system as a mother with child and therefore has an income of her own. This is the way of life for those in the welfare system and it is a circle that very rarely gets broken. For a boy that hits that age he has to either get a job somewhere or earn money illegally. The choice of preference is the drug trade.

Food stamps are a good idea except when they are used for anything but food. They should come as a debit card with a picture I.D. and considering that ninety-nine percent of all stores that sell food have a bar code scanner, only acceptable food products should be allowed to be charged to the food stamp debit card. If anyone were caught misusing it there should be considerable jail time.

My friend the plumber has told me that there are local programs that are county wide that are there to help those in the county that are having a hard time making ends meet. Some of the recipients are elderly and some are truly physically challenged and need this financial help, such as oil or gas for heating in the winter months. There are those that are just plain lazy and shouldn't receive this handout without any strings attached. My personal point of view is that if you are receiving help from any of these programs you should be doing community services for those who can't do things for themselves. If you are too lazy to do so, then you shouldn't receive financial aid!

Whenever I drive down a road or street I see garbage along the side of the road, I see side walks and playgrounds that could be better maintained. I see roads and streets with potholes and disrepair. I see homes of low income elderly and even the government owned hosing in need of routine maintenance. There is so much out there that could be done and should be done by those with their hand out and wanting something for nothing. Get something and give something, show initiative and make yourself more attractive in searching for a job. Anyone who can show initiative to go above and beyond what is expected of them is a very hirable individual for any company.

Earn your way in life and stop using the excuse that society has created the problem and owes you a living. On the flip of a coin, Local, State, and Federal government, including the wealthy should take a cut in pay and create jobs for those who need them. If those that receive these jobs don't put an honest effort in performing the tasks of these jobs, then they get no welfare. It is as simple as that!

While we're on the subject of Government payments, let me give you my thoughts on Social Security. When it was first implemented in 1935, it was a good idea to at least allow an elderly person who worked their whole life to at least have some form of a retirement and a little bit of income to help live on. The problem is that throughout the decades as the "Baby Boomers" began to enter the work force and paying into Social Security, the "Pot" grew big, and the government figured it could use some of that money towards other programs. Basically, they took our hard earned "Nest Egg" and screwed us over. During one Presidential Election Campaign the candidates made a big issue of that when the Baby Boomers became eligible for Social Security there wouldn't be anything left in the "Pot" to pay out. So, some even had the audacity to suggest that we should be allowed to put our Social Security Taxes we normally pay in and invest it into the market.

Now let me remind you that the Stock Market is just another legal form of gambling. And also let me remind you again why we are in a severe recession. I've heard of some stupid ideas before, although letting our government handle our retirement fund is pretty stupid, but the party that came up with this one needs a good kick in the ass.

Now, they come up with another bright idea that the age of collecting Social Security should be raised from Sixty-five years old to Sixty-eight or even Seventy years of age. I have been in the work force since Sixteen years old, which if I retire at age Sixty-five, I would have been working for Forty-nine years. Technically, if you add in the mowing lawns and racking leaves for relatives I have been in the work force much longer. Not everyone has worked in an office most of their life. Many have physically worked their ass off and deserve to retire at Sixty-five if they so chose without being penalized!

So, to those elected officials who are in charge of Social Security, leave the God Damned thing alone and put back what you took out of it, and not with "We the People's" money. You spent it without our consent, you pay it back!

The Illegal Drug Trade

THIS IS SOMETHING I know a decent amount about. I have seen "Coke Queens", "Crack Whores", "Pushers", "Dealers", "Mules", "Double Dealers", "Plants", "Chasers", the list goes on and on and on. The average person has only a small idea of what goes on inside the world of drug trafficking. The common recreational user thinks that they are "Hip" and talk a good bullshit line around their friends, but throw them into the deep crap amongst the gangs and the crack houses and they would fearfully shit their pants and start crying. On the flip of the coin the hard cases do not know any better and are too stupid and arrogant to know what they are doing to their life and all of those they affect.

The only good it does is it has added to the element of human destruction. Remember that we as an animal specie has taken away all the threats of nature's natural enemies to human kind, except for one, which is Man Himself! We have far surpassed all other predators when we learned to build weapons of destruction. So, in the scheme of things, deaths due to the involvement of illegal drugs have become one of our few predatory enemies. It not only seeks the guilty, but the innocent as well.

In the Sixties and Seventies, it was a cultural thing. The Peace Movement was going on and the youth of wealthy nations were revolting against the repression, of war, and suppressed ideas of a peaceful society of equality. When the drug cloud lifted the protesting youth either had died of drug overdoses or they learned that to survive in this world you have to conform into what is expected of you. The drugs never went away, just the ideology of it all. Corporate America and the World's Wealth only were biding their time for it to fizzle out. Patience is indeed a virtue!

In the mid Eighties and beyond the up coming youth rebelled in a different way, they escaped reality by slipping into the drug cloud. Corporate America accepted it for awhile as going with the flow, but got wise again and re-shifted their policies back in the late Nineties. Gangs also took the initiative and dominated the selling end of it during this period as well.

It is amazing how times keep repeating itself over and over! First, we had the battles and wars over the wealth of land, its waters, its timbers and fertile soil. Later it was still over the acquisition of land, but for its gold and silver. Next came oil, and still is over oil, but in the silent forefront and in its light shadowy background it has been for the wealth of drugs that battles are truly fought. Ask any DEA Agent or Drug Taskforce of your local Police Department. It's our youth that are what is at stake here, and again, no one cares as long as it is not affecting their "Comfort Zone".

At one point in our recent past, one of our Presidents declared "War on Drugs", but it wasn't much of a war considering no one remembers it. We captured a major pain in the ass called Manuel Noriega, but there is more to that and I am not at liberty to discuss it.

We finally have gotten somewhere in Colombia, though cocaine still comes from there, but is being grown and manufactured around the world also to fill the demand. Heroin has made a comeback and is grown and processed all over the world as well, with thanks to the previous administration for the war on terror and resurgence of Middle Eastern Heroin.

Pot has made a strong comeback, especially when it was legalized for medical purposes. My thoughts on this are that if tobacco products are still legal, then why not for true medicinal purposes. I don't believe that it should be legalized for recreational reasons.

As I have stated, I was involved in the drug trade many years ago and Marijuana does have a strong tendency to lead to other stronger drugs. If you are one of those who states that it doesn't then you are only bullshitting yourself and anyone else that is that stupid to believe you. I spent fifteen years of my life in and around drugs and have seen a seventy-five percent trade off of those who started out on pot and worked their way into using harder drugs. It starts out as only slipping out of reality and worries just a tiny bit, and next thing you find out you are getting higher on heavier stuff because reality seems to get worse.

Remember this, Ignorance can be corrected, but Stupidity is with you forever!!! Once stupid, always stupid!!! Act stupid, get treated as stupid!!!

The problem with Humans and today's society is that some users and dealers are ignorant and can be rehabilitated to a point, but there are far more that are completely stupid and can never be. This unfortunately is a simple fact of life and you only need to travel in the right places to see this. Once a Coke Queen or a Crack Whore, always a Coke Queen or a Crack Whore!!! The temptation will always be there for you to slip a little.

What can be done you ask? Well for one thing we need much tougher punishments. Those who deal or traffic the hard drugs, Coke, Heroin, Crack, Crystal Meth, Ecstasy, and Over the Counter Pain Killers should spend life in prison with no parole, and if your state has a death penalty then go for it. If this seems too drastic and severe, then tell me what is the difference between a serial killer and someone who sells drugs that have the capability of taking someone's life away actually or figuratively? It would be like someone with a revolver half loaded and playing "Russian Roulette" with their victims. Sooner or later someone <u>will die</u>!

Those who are only users should face fifteen to life because they are endangering all of those around them, just like a suicide bomber. When the addict is high are coming down and needs a fix they will lie, cheat, steal, and even kill for another high. Like leaving your child with a babysitter who's a pedophile! Nothing good will ever come of it!

As far as I'm concerned, tobacco products should be banned as well. With all of the information that is out there today of how bad and deathly dangerous tobacco products are it completely amazes me of how actually stupid people are who smoke. It is filthy and disgusting and it is not "cool" to see. It only shows how pathetic that person is, and I don't want to hear how hard it is to quit. The human mind is as powerful to stop an addiction as it is to keep an addict addicted. Again, it only proves my point about world politics and that if huge profits can be made, Big Business will get away with murder!!!

If you think what I have just suggested is severe, then you will really like this next one. Anyone else involved in the sale, trafficking, or use of any other lesser illegal narcotic should go through a month of daily electrical shock therapy of the hands and feet! Let's face it, if you slap a child's hands often enough they will eventually stop reaching into the cookie jar when they are not suppose to! I grew up in farm country and watched farm animals stay away from the electric fence. Again, ignorance can be corrected, but stupidity is with you the rest of your life!

For those parents that don't seem to have control of their children I have a very special thing to say to you. I am not only talking to those single parents that have one or several children that are involved in gangs, but I am also talking to all of those parents that have been so loose with their children that they have no idea that their darling little angels are playing bully and/or getting high and drunk and getting into all kinds of trouble with the law. You can't make false threats because sooner or later your kid will call your bluff. You can't wait till they are in their mid teens to try discipline either, it has to start when they can understand the words yes and no.

Now I don't mean to beat your child either. My children knew when I only pointed my finger to the corner, it meant they had misbehaved and they were to sit in the corner until it was time to have a discussion about why they had misbehaved and why mommy and daddy didn't approve of it. A child is small and has a very big imagination and it helps to install a little fear into that imagination of what a parent might do. Have you ever noticed animal parents in the wild and how they teach their children about living in the wild? There is no difference in the wild and in human society. None of us parents want our children to die homeless in the streets.

My biggest belief is that Parents should be punished as well when their children commit a crime. I will go out on a limb and state that the very large majority of the time when a child has committed a crime, or at least something really bad and disrespectful it can be traced back to the parents as either the parents attitude, or lack of discipline, or lack of knowing or caring what their child is doing, or all of the above. So, therefore, punish the child and punish the parent or parents equally. I bet if this starts to take place parents will be more responsible on how they are raising their children and there will be less juvenile crimes as well!!!

As a parent you have taken a very big responsibility to have and raise a child. If you were not willing to accept this responsibility then you should have kept your legs together or tied a knot in it instead. For those parents that are separated, divorced, or just flat out abandoned your responsibility, then you still should suffer the consequences for you child's misbehavior and do the same punishment as well. Your child your responsibility! Even if it isn't your child, but the child lives under the same roof as you and you have taken on the responsibility of raising them on your own or at least help to raise them you need to accept the responsibility fully under the law.

A child is only a reflection of the parent or parents. How many times have you caught yourself not wanting to make the same mistakes as your parents did in your eyes, but made them anyway? Our youth are our legacy. They are our future for mankind. Think of them as the last handful of seeds you have left and how precious they are, to see to it that they are planted, nurtured, kept growing healthy, to sustain your life and memory. You bet your ass you better hold yourself responsible and accountable for their sake!!!

Our Government's Debt

THE AVERAGE PERSON who runs their credit cards to the max, with no possible means to be able to pay their debt off, all of you would agree is out of control. They usually are denied loans from lending institutions, the companies that hold their credit cards that are maxed out usually resort to bringing that person to claims court in order to try to get payment in some form, and the person owing all of that money has fallen into financial despair. Sounds familiar?

It should sound familiar because that just basically described our wonderful Government! Think of credit card over spending as our Government borrowing from other countries to pay for everything our Government spends money on. We, as tax payers send to the government a portion of what we claim to earn in the form of taxes we owe. To our Government this is money earned by them to supply programs like Medicaid, Welfare, Unemployment Benefits (though businesses also pay into the government towards this), our Military and National Security, Maintaining Infrastructure (roads and bridges), Research, Maintaining our National Parks and Landmarks, Wages and Salaries of Government Officials and their Staff, and the list goes on and on. Businesses also pay taxes as well, though some large corporations pay less than their share because of incentives given to them from moving their businesses elsewhere in the world. We also pay into our Government, either to our State and/or our National Government, taxes on fuel, clothing, food, property, vehicle, and even utilities. All these taxes we as a people of the United States pay in, really have no clue as to just how much is spent where and why so much is spent. We never see any accountability!

Think of our Government as a huge corporation, with our President and Vice President as the CEO's, our Congress and Senate as the Board of Trustees, and "We the People" are share holders. Like a corporation we as share holders have the right to elect our government, though we actually don't elect our President and Vice President.

Now I want all of you who are reading this think about what I am going to state next, and think about Enron, Citibank, Fannie Mae and Freddie Mac, AIG, IndyMac, all of those banks that were about to go bankrupt but were too big to fail, Chrysler and GM's Bailout, and all of those billions of dollars were given out with "No Strings Attached"! Now to me I do not see any accountability here. Would a bank lend you any money with no strings attached? Hell No! Why did our Government do so? Sure, Enron got a few slaps in the face, but the investors who invested their life savings got screwed big time. One would believe that our tax dollars that we pay for "protection against criminals" would protect us from them, but not so. "Oh Well, such is life".

So, during this banking crisis in 2008, what does our Government do, it allows the cheap take over of Merrill Lynch by Bank of America, Washington Mutual to JP Morgan Chase, and Bear Stearns to JP Morgan Chase after the Government agreed to lend Bear Stearns $29 billion. Who got it shoved up the ass big time? WE the People, that's who!

We as average taxpayers give around a fourth of our hard earned money to our Government. We expect them to do the best thing with our money that is in our best interests. We would like to see our Congress and Senate, our President and Vice President hold themselves accountable to us as taxpayers, since "We the Taxpayers" are where the money comes from. Yes, all businesses pay in taxes as well and you would expect the same accountability, but most of those businesses' employees are regular taxpayers as are you and me.

When a government gives the financial institutions in its boundaries free reins like they did in the Nineteen-nineties, and these same financial institutions take advantage of this opportunity and stick it to the American People, the taxpayers, our Government on our behalf should have been a little smarter and <u>Not</u> give these same financial institutions bailout money with no strings attached, without any accountability. When these same failing financial institutions gave some of their higher paid employees' huge bonuses, it sounds to me that this was for acknowledgement for "Getting Away With It" and screwing the American Taxpayer even more!

It appears to me that the financial institutions hurt Americans even more than the 911 attacks ever did. We attacked Afghanistan and Iraq, why are we letting the financial institutions getting away with what they did?

I feel a little sorry for those who received mortgages to buy homes and in reality couldn't really afford them, especially when they had signed up for a mortgage that sounded affordable until the balloon payment part took affect. The banks knew what they were doing, but morally shouldn't have done it.

The mortgagors should have done their "homework" as well. They should have sat done and figured out what they could sensibly afford before jumping into something they couldn't. As I stated I feel a "little" sorry for them, but not that much. Not everyone is a math and financial wiz, but please, stop being stupid. If you want the Government to hold themselves accountable, then you need to hold yourself accountable as well. Your "Comfort Zone" may get stretched one way or the other, but you are human and can adapt.

Those who bought their home before the recession, and are struggling to make their mortgage payments need help. Think about it for a moment. Let's say you bought a home in Nineteen-ninety-five for $300,000.00. It was appraised at that price then, and now you would be lucky to sell it for $175,000.00. If the bank forecloses on you and ends up selling it at an auction and only gets $150,000.00 for it, it seems to me that they would be better off letting you keep the mortgage and lessen the payments and the interest percentage you are paying. Then, when your financial situation improves, payment amounts and interest percentage should go up as well. After all, it is usually the greed of the financial institutions that causes these recessions and so they should take some of the losses as do the rest of us have to. Its no different than with the situation that Towns, Cities, States, and the Federal Government are going through with the Unions and the Cadillac Packages that are now so fiercely being re-negotiated over. The times have changed and we all have to adapt to the new situation whether we like it or not. Everyone has to, not just We the People.

Number one; the banks should never accept a contract to lend a person any money for a home, nor should a person borrowing any money for such, unless that contract payment is not more than a certain percentage of what the borrower makes. In other words, a certain percentage of your pay goes to housing, for food, for clothing, for transportation, for healthcare, for a retirement plan, with a certain percentage for personal expenses. Whatever that percentage for shelter is, you as a borrower and the bank as a lender should not go over that limit. It also wouldn't hurt to cut back little to give a little room for economic down turns.

Its time "We the People" take back our Government somehow, someway, and possibly in some shape or form. Our Government started out with somewhat good intentions, but it keeps getting more and more out of control. We as a people of these modern times are not as ignorant as our ancestors were about our governmental workings. Our Government is much too big and instead of drastically cutting budgets that are essential to our being able to live at least a little more comfortable, we need to modify them. Find out where the waste spending is taking place in each of these programs and policies, and eliminate the waste. We need to start from A to Z and go through each and every policy. Our Government needs to go through everything with a fine tooth comb, what it spends money on and eliminate what it doesn't need. If there are departments that have more employees than there is actual work for, then those extra employees need to be transferred to another department where they are needed or let go. Personally, when there is time for "horseplay", or bullshit sessions, hours in a week spent that are more fraternizing than being productive at your job, then you are not busy and there are too many employees doing the work that fewer employees can do efficiently. Yes we are not machines, but non productivity is wasteful and a burden on us taxpayers.

For the money we spend on research are we getting our money's worth, or are we getting good accountability. Are we funding research for stupid things that have no benefit or gain except to give out excess funding money to meet a budget? Over the years I have heard the News Media come out with some form of a stupid and wasteful idea our government is funding. Personally, the person or group of people responsible for allowing this to be funded should be "bitch slapped" and fired! Period!

Instead of arguing over it and coming up with funding extensions after extensions, why doesn't our Government Policy Makers use some common sense and pass a budget that is financially moral and feasible? I strongly feel that if they can not do this, then we, as the taxpaying majority should be allowed to fire all of them immediately, force them to pay back to the government all of their salaries, times four, that they were paid while wasting our time, and quickly elect those who say they can! Let the budget stay as it is and if the next group of elected officials can't do it either, fire them under the same terms and find another group, so on and so forth. Eventually, odds are we will find a group of law makers that will hold themselves accountable to us, the taxpayers, the ones who come up with the money year after year to pay their salaries.

Who are The Tea Party Movement

THE TEA PARTY Movement came about during the campaigning for the Presidency in Two Thousand and Seven. It became stronger after President Obama was elected and added a somewhat fourth or fifth party to American politics. They basically are Republican Conservatives acting out to a degree of what I am proposing, except, they aren't really changing a thing. They like the system that is in place where as "We the People" are just a flock of scared sheep and the Government is our Sheppard who keeps us safe and fed. The original "Boston Tea Party" was enacted by a group of Colonists who were tired of paying excessively high taxes to English Government and Monarchy.

May I remind you that tea drinking during Colonial times was more afforded by the wealthier citizens of the colonies rather than the poor majority of laborers who earned barely enough to survive? They even tried to pass the blame onto Native Americans, whom had nothing to do with it.

Basically, the Tea Party Movement is based on the actions of wealthier minorities rebelling against an injustice to their way of life. So basically, the Tea Party Movement is the same type of people that dumped the tea into Boston Harbor in 1773, with a few "follow along groupies" that haven't a real clue what the hell they are standing for. Remember my thoughts about the Revolutionary War?

What I propose is a complete Government overhaul, from top to bottom. I think the playing field should be leveled to make things fair for all, and I mean all. We are not a Socialist or Communistic Society and shouldn't be fed propaganda that we are free. We shouldn't be paying taxes to a Government that can't and won't hold themselves completely accountable, right to the penny, to what they are spending our hard earned dollars on. That's why we are in the dire situation we are in economically.

Our Government is way too big and those that we supposedly put in charge of running it need to stop treating their elected jobs as an elite club. Our Government needs to be made much smaller. I'm sure that there are an over abundance of positions that could be done away with. These positions could be done by the rest of the staff. Our Nation is in serious trouble and it is primarily their fault. It is their entire fault, not just the President, past or present, or the Congress, or the Senate. It isn't either the Democrats or the Republicans; the blame is on all of them. We put them there to look out for our best interests and look at the mess they made of it!

At times it is like hearing a bunch of children arguing and pointing fingers on a play ground. Personally, I would like to slap all of them in the back of the head and tell them to grow up. Start acting rationally and do what is truly good for the people and not what is best for your own wallets. An elected office should be a privilege to serve and represent all of the American People, not an acceptance to an elite country club where you only represent the wealthy and throw a small bone to the majority common citizens. When there are extremely important issues to be decided, they shouldn't be taking vacations, rather knuckle down and get the job done correctly. Those same important issues should be finalized by a vote by We the People, considering we can't trust you whom we elect to do the right thing to start with.

We are not stupid, ignorant, or uneducated to the point that we can not comprehend the truth of how the world works and are unable to determine what we really need and want for survival. It is about time we stand up for our rights to be a free society of peoples, living under one nation, governed by our own majority of people, holding ourselves accountable for our actions as well as our own truly elected government "Of The People, By The People, and For The People of the United States Of America"! It is time we stand as one and let the world take notice. If they can do it in North Africa and in the Middle East, then why can't we!

A Final Note

A LOT HAS happened since the first concept of putting together this manuscript. We as a Nation are so far indebt to China and other countries that our grandchildren, and possibly our great grandchildren may not see the light of day. Our politicians refuse to agree on the necessary means to resolve this problem. They keep waiting to the final minute of every deadline and still, they can't resolve our problems. Republicans refuse to allow the wealthy to pay more taxes. Democrats refuse to make cuts to Welfare. Personally, I deeply feel that we are in the beginning stages of the fall of the Great Empire known as the United States of America, and it is a proven fact that all empires fall within the average of 200 years.

We have a President who came into office when the "Shit Hit the Fan" and he tried to get both sides to do their jobs and come to some compromise and save our Nation from ruin, but to no avail. We can't make China bring the value of its currency up to realistic value because they have us "by the balls". They own us.

Sooner or later Iran will be manufacturing their own nuclear weapons and our military is so spread thin and we as a Nation can't afford another war front, and because of that we really don't have a military option as a bargaining chip, while the United Nations sits idly by.

"Occupy Wall Street" has taken place and it shows that although it is only a few thousand people that are there protesting, there are a few million of us that aren't there, but want Wall Street to stop being so damn greedy. Even though there are those that live in the areas where the protesting is taking place are angry with the protestors, there are the majority of Americans that want change. We keep hearing promises by those who seek election, but they are empty promises. It hasn't changed since our Government became into being.

The occupiers should realize that no one can camp out and spend the night in any park, unless it is a designated camp ground. The Middle East has led the way for us to follow. They didn't camp out in parks, rather they banned together and helped each other with shelter, food and water, but many have died over there for the sake of freedom. For those Mayors and Police Officers, National Guards, keep in mind all that happened at Kent State on May 4, 1970. We the People want a big change with our government.

Again, I have to remind myself of the fact that Humans only care about the world around them for a little while, until they are distracted by something else. Most of us Americans have adjusted our "Comfort Zone" with compromise and are getting use to this lower standard of comfort, but we still are not completely comfortable.

In Retrospect

I MAY SEEM to you to be a bit of a complainer, a "Grumpy Old Man" so to say, but somewhere in my writings I had to have gotten your thoughts of approval or at least some consideration. Whether you agree with me or disagree, the world would be a better place if all sides were equal. Ideas I have proposed could be a building block, or a starting point to build a great nation from, or a world for that matter. We would be a planet of people with no hunger, no prejudice, and no greed, no wealthy and no poor. Everyone would work hard for the good of our planet. We wouldn't be over populated and there would be plenty of room for nature to still be wild. There wouldn't be any propaganda forced on us and stating "we are free" when we are not.

Yes we are in some ways better off than most around the world, but we are lied to, deceived, and herded like sheep and cattle, just as those others are. We are not stupid or illiterate. We as a people are intelligent enough to know right and wrong and enough so to make rational and fair decisions to better the world around us overall if we are given all of the correct information to start with, with no fancy words that need a law degree to decipher. When a people stand together, united in a cause, as awful as it seems, if we all stand united, they can't kill us all! Who will do the work that they feel is beneath them? As nature has so many times proven a fact of life, the strongest will prevail. Stand together and speak out!

So, remember this very important thought. No matter how or why you go about your life, with everything that you think, say, do, and feel, there is always a little bit of the Grumpy Old Man, or Woman, inside all of us.

Thank you very much for your time.

Sincerely, The Grumpy Old Man